C000295115

Reviews for
Nine Lives and Counting

"*Nine Lives and Counting* is a thoughtfully crafted memoir, populated with humor and insight."

"The universalities of human life resting deep in us all are drawn out for reflection. The search for confidence and purpose . . . and the complex world of love, family, and friends resonate. Sit down with *Nine Lives and Counting* and be inspired as John finds inner courage and turns the ordinary into the fascinating."

—Dr. Lisa P. Turner, author of *Dream Take Flight*

"In this book, the reader journeys with John's physical and emotional abuse of being bullied and tormented from a young age through the teens and extending into the twenties. As you continue to read, his tenacity and courage pop up through the many adventures he has experienced. In his life events, he shares himself and how he courageously lives to overcome adversities to be able to change his lifestyle. Discover yourself in the pages of *Nine Lives and Counting.*"

—Helen Damon Hesketh, author of *Born Unwanted*

"A brilliant memoir that captures the life of a truly brilliant man from different parts of the globe, from the highs to the lows, I almost felt I was there with him. I couldn't keep my eyes off the page sentence after sentence... Fantastic!"

—Kieran Robertson

"This book was such a delight. *Nine Lives and Counting* should be essential reading for those looking for history, travel, adventure, romance, or anyone who loves reading amazing classics. John is an exceptional writer and *Nine Lives and Counting* is a book that will never become obsolete."

"Nine Lives and Counting is John's exciting and interesting memoir. The author introduces his readers to different chapters of his powerful life. Ranging from a stressful time in Vietnam to when traveling and living the dream. Throughout the book, John is incredibly and sometimes amusingly cutting about various friends, former colleagues and family. As a young man, he embarks on a journey of self-discovery with surprising results.

"I found this book to be very well thought out and well written. It also teaches a lesson of morals. No matter what life throws at you, you always have the power to bounce back and continue. John shows us that this is possible. His narrative voice is wonderful, he is serious at times but also very witty, which makes for an engaging read. It feels absolutely real, as though I'm reading someone's actual journal. John has many wonderful insights on life. I definitely recommend this book to other readers."

—Shantel Orkoz

"It didn't take long to realize this book is not just another memoir. The author had the unusual ability to relate the emotions and perspective of a young child (with his earliest experience being the wartime blitz in London and subsequent boarding school experiences), and yet convey these experiences with just the right amount of cynicism, even seven decades later. Then quite interesting reading was his fresh perspective of different aspects of American society—not only as a recent immigrant, but also an inductee into its Army.

"Just when I was fascinated by that, John is off again to another war—Vietnam. I found his unique perspective of that conflict with all its cultural differ-ence and moral ambiguity of some of its participants very fascinating reading. Nothing is sugar-coated; he describes his encounters with the dark side uniquely, even after his return to America and his descriptions of the struggles he overcomes. This was one of the very few nonfiction books that I was not able to put down until the end."

—Peter Kurschner

"*Nine Lives and Counting* took me on a roller coaster of emotions, not felt in a long time. John's incredible journey made me feel that I was part of it. This book is like a wake-up call to us all, to live life to the full. There were times when I wanted to put the book down, but my fingers kept turning the pages. I would definitely recommend reading this book."

—Mike Daniel

"This memoir is as much about the surroundings and events of John's young life as it is about him. And that is a perspective, particularly of the Second World War in England, from the eyes of a toddler. The author has no idea of the world, except as it is. It is the norm. So, as John matures, and things change, as he changes, the perspective changes, becoming more worldly. It is the evolution of the person that keeps us interested. A gut-wrenching, life-changing, and suspenseful memoir that kept my attention until the very last page."

—Bob Rich, author of *The Miami River*

NINE LIVES
AND COUNTING

NINE LIVES
AND COUNTING

A Memoir of Adventure,
Self-Discovery and Bouncing Back

JOHN P. CULNANE

Cover Design: Pagatana Design Service
Book Interior and E-book Design: Amit Dey
Production & Publishing Consultant: Geoff Affleck
Proofreading: Nina Shoroplova

ISBN: 978-1-8380670-0-7 (Paperback)
ISBN: 978-1-8380670-1-4 (eBook)

1. BIO026000 BIOGRAPHY & AUTOBIOGRAPHY / Personal Memoirs
2. BIO008000 BIOGRAPHY & AUTOBIOGRAPHY / Military
3. BIO025000 BIOGRAPHY & AUTOBIOGRAPHY / Editors, Journalists, Publishers
4. BIO038000 BIOGRAPHY & AUTOBIOGRAPHY / Survival

Author's Note

The events in this memoir are true to the best of my memory, though some of the dialogue has been reconstructed for dramatic effect. The names of some individuals have been changed and, in some cases, identifiable information has been altered to protect their identities.

Acknowledgments

Danny DeCillis, PhD, as a developmental editor, has an absolute mastery of words; he knows what makes a text tick. Under his constant guidance and endless hours, my manuscript has evolved, from being a rough draft to be a highly polished book ready for publishing; he is also a pleasure to work with.

Geoff Affleck, publishing consultant and author of *5 Things Every First-Time Author Needs to Know*, with his unrivaled expertise in the field of publishing. I thank him and his team of designers, typesetters, and SEO specialists, for their input, professionalism, and attention to every minute detail. When you cross bridges or meet a fork in the road, it's always good to know that the way is clear straight ahead without obstacles. Geoff always makes sure that happens. Geoff is the go-to publishing professional to have on your team when you are only satisfied with the best.

Contents

Foreword xv

Preface xvii

Part 1: Great Britain 1

My father, the stranger 6

My mother, the trooper 17

My family, in all its glory 21

Lesson 1: The sadistic nuns of Bridport 24

Lesson 2: The cruel cadets and bully
  boys of Holbrook 32

Lesson 3: Don't drink the sacramental wine. . .36

Lesson 4: Morden Technical and discovering
  girls 42

Lesson 5: Girls who liked to drink, smoke
  and dance 45

The last lesson: What do I want to be when
  I grow up? 47

Part 2: America **49**

Crossing the pond without getting my feet wet . . 49

Learning the new language! 51

When "Uncle Sam" speaks, you listen 52

"Yes, Sir". 53

Showing the US Army how to shoot 59

I'm in charge now 62

Saying goodbye to the US Army 64

Part 3: Vietnam **67**

Asia beckons: plentiful and delicious food
    and girls 67

Someone has to do the dirty work, but it
    won't be me 70

Murder and suicide: All in a night's work 73

Looking down the barrel of a .45 78

How to live in a war zone without getting
    your head blown off 81

Be careful how you choose your friends 86

"I promise you won't feel a thing; I'm just
    going to cut your leg off." 87

Whatever love is. 89

Part 4: America. **91**

University: Study time or party time? 96

Do what you have to do and don't look back . .97

It helps if you love what you do 100

Be careful when you turn your back 104

A dream job with less than dream pay. 105

When you climb a ladder, make sure you
　　trust the person holding it 108

What you write could last forever, so choose
　　your words wisely 113

The US Veterans Hospital saved my life. . . . 119

The final chapter of my American story 122

Part 5: The World Is My Oyster **125**

Just buy a ticket and go 126

"Wrong John" 128

How the other half lives 138

Part 6: Choices **145**

How much did you say you drink? 145

What makes a survivor? 146

Foreword

Sometimes, a memoir by Citizen X, an unknown, unfamous, unrepentant human being living amongst billions of Citizen Xs, is more riveting than a 1000-page memoir by a well-known, well-borne, and well-loved or hated figure of importance.

John Culnane's pithy personal history, *Nine Lives and Counting*, recounts horrific and tender events with equal humorous and tragic weight, from childhood atrocities in Dickensian nun-run boarding schools where vomit bowls are used as serving utensils and boys grow sprouts under drain pipes so as not to starve—to moments in faraway fantasy lands in cocaine, gun-crazed Miami where drunken, bawdy joke-telling with ill-tempered Irish monsignors carries on while incompetent low-level bureaucrats plot to overthrow the author with the vengeance of a third-world coup.

On hearing John tell his life story, his friend Rachel says that since "always wrong" John never married or had children, he would go "extinct." This makes John extraordinarily sad. But the pages of memories Culnane scribes in this compelling personal history will ensure that a part of him will live on in the DNA of his words, which are true, deep and funny, as we follow him doing daily battle, an ordinary hero going up against ordinary villains like landlords who steal bottles of Chivas Regal and .45 pistols, and end up murdering wives, with bits blown about the floor like "chicken bones."

Culnane bounces through life from job to job, relationship to relationship, neurotic observation to neurotic observation, never resisting the curveballs that knock him in the gut, and even almost kill him at times. This is what his memoir imparts to us. Rather than wallow in past crimes perpetuated upon him by other humans and life, from wars in Vietnam with the Viet Cong on muddy AK-47 laden roads to battles in suburban Miami hi-rise apartment buildings with painters who chronically steal paint, Culnane chooses to live with joy, resilience, and laughter.

As Harvey Pekar, the great comic book writer of the "American Splendor" series once said: "Ordinary life is pretty complex stuff." Culnane truly lives this remarkable, small saying as we experience his *Nine Lives and Counting* in his small but expansive memoir. There are so many dark voids in Culnane's life, but what he manages to do is point the way forward for us when we slip into our own dark holes: Live with the humorous courage, forgive those who hurt you, and carry on with that perennial British stiff upper lip.

—Duba Leibell,
Producer, Screenplay writer,
Professor in the Film Department at
University of Miami

Preface

On a rain-drenched small windy island located off the North Atlantic coast, a lone writer sits at his computer and writes into the night. The island is Great Britain, the writer is John P. Culnane. His self-imposed task: to write his memoirs, to bring his readers on an emotional trip that causes them to question the meaning of their lives.

Great intro, huh? It sounds like the beginning of a movie. But that suits me because my life has been a lot like a movie too. In the many decades of my life, I have lived a real roller-coaster ride spanning a bunch of different jobs and adventures over three continents. So much so that you might wonder how so much could happen to one person; perhaps I'm the cat with nine lives.

Why bother, you may ask? Why tell my story? It's true—I'm neither famous nor noteworthy. I have, however, lived through a great deal. During my lifelong quest for novelty and change, I've learned skills ranging from flying a plane to martial arts to pipe organ building. I've been shot at by the Viet Cong, backstabbed by business associates, and navigated situations filled with danger. I haven't always come out on top, but I've survived it all, and I've usually found a way to turn the tables to my advantage.

I won't lie—it's been a hard journey, and it almost ended up badly, when the alcohol and cancer nearly got the best of me. But thanks to some skilled doctors, my determination to turn things around, and a little luck, I've gotten the chance to come home to Great Britain and reflect on my life. I think, all things considered, it's an incredible story, and telling it is worthwhile. We all have stories. Sit down with one of your favorite old aunts or uncles, give them a glass of sherry, and just listen. I guarantee you will run out of sherry before they run out of stories.

There's a reason why we tell these stories: when we don't tell others about our lives, a lot gets lost. That aunt or uncle has priceless family history in their heads. I've got just as many stories as any of them, but I won't be telling my tales with sherry; I've learned the hard way that too much alcohol doesn't help in telling a coherent story. Or in living a coherent life, for that matter. But more about that later.

Once, while working as a journalist for a news magazine, I interviewed a businesswoman. When I asked her to tell me about herself, she asked what I wanted to know. "Everything," I said. She looked at me for a moment and then started laughing. This wasn't the way most interviews started. But from then on, she poured out her guts to me, and her story really sprang to life. She later told me, after the article was published, that her story resonated with so many people that her business improved.

It wasn't my intention to help increase her sales, but the reading public liked her story. Her struggle for success was relatable, and people rallied to support her. It transformed her from a businessperson to a person. She shared a lot of herself in this story, and as a result, she got a lot back.

What this made me realize is that if you give a lot, you will often get unexpected returns, and that telling your story is a powerful thing.

Writing this book has brought me face to face again with a lot of the dark times in my life. The bad stuff is still there, and occasionally, I will go to those dark places—but the on-off switch in my brain is programmed to not dwell on negative thoughts. As a result, despite the sometimes harrowing things I've lived through, I'm not generally haunted by demons from my past. And on the other side, I have vivid memories of the good times. They're all there, to be revisited whenever I want, and that's made it all worthwhile.

As with any good story, I've left stuff out. It wasn't my intention for you to read this book to fall asleep. I have left out the parts where I was making pizza, delivering pizza, and eating the undeliverable pizzas. I left out the monotonous hours I spent counting millions of dollars in a bank vault. I left out the endless miles I traveled as a driver. You get the point. But I included most of the good bits.

Maybe it will help you. Maybe it won't. But I must think that there are some lessons to be learned from what I've been through. And even if you don't learn a thing, at least you ought to find it a good story, sherry or no sherry.

PART 1

Great Britain

L et's pull back the curtain and look at my dramatic entrance into this world. I was born in a private clinic in Sheffield, Great Britain. Doctors were in short supply because of the war effort, so there wasn't one in the house when I arrived. This was a little dangerous, because—as my mother told me years later—sometimes the cord gets twisted and insufficient oxygen gets through to jump-start the baby, which is what happened to me. I was born a "blue baby," or a baby starved of oxygen.

I only just made it. It seems like I was a survivor from the beginning; nothing was going to prevent me from entering this world.

My mother, Helen Culnane, had a special mission one early summer morning. She carefully wrapped her package and walked deliberately to the local butcher shop in the leafy suburb of Barnes, London.

"I see you've brought it," said the butcher.

"It's not an it," replied my mother, slightly offended. "It's my son."

The butcher shook his head.

"Hurry up and weigh him before the customers come in," he said gruffly.

My mother took me to the butcher to get weighed because homes didn't have scales anymore: they'd all been requisitioned for military use. I was born in the middle of World War II, and life in England was hard. Every household had to do its part, and that mostly meant giving the government whatever it wanted. And the government wanted a lot. Everyone's aluminum pots and pans, in excess, were taken and melted down for the war effort. If you were fortunate enough to be rich and possessed lots of expensive copper pans, the man from the ministry took those also—thank you very much. You were left with what the man from the ministry thought was enough, and that, of course, was never enough. Wartime London, and the rest of the UK, was just like that.

Even though I was incredibly young, I can remember pieces of the heavy plaster and wood lathed ceiling falling in our kitchen as a result of aircraft bomb activity. My mother and I would then go out the next day and look at whatever house got hit. Our house wasn't hit directly, of course, or I wouldn't be telling you this story.

Wartime entertainment was scarce, and we weren't rich. I didn't spend my youngest years going to zoos and places like that. Instead my mother would take me to Barnes Common where the anti-aircraft gunners were positioned. Scattered around, all over the ground, were long brass casings from the anti-aircraft guns.

When the gunners weren't looking, I would scoop up a handful and take them home as trophies. Although most of the casings were supposed to be melted down and the brass reused for the war effort, plenty made it into homes, carried in pockets like mine. This is why some of it was used in ornaments you can still find here and there. It wasn't until years later that I discovered that my family was living next to a factory heavily involved in the war effort, "Beverley Works" in Barnes. It was no wonder that bombs were falling nearby.

John. Barnes, London, 1947 age 5½.

Nothing was ever enough. Ration books only covered necessities of minuscule quantities. People had to make do with whatever they could get. If you saw a woman strolling around with a new fur collar, chances were it had recently been a pet cat. Nobody cared or paid attention unless it was *their* cat. And then if it had been their cat, shame on them for allowing it to slip away, be eaten, and have its fur used on someone's coat; this was wartime—nothing was wasted.

There were more important things to deal with than missing pets—such as staying alive with the bombs raining down. The government told us all that the correct use of blackout curtains was considered critical, and people did their best to comply. But no bomber was going to drop a bomb just because they saw a light on; they had a mission, and only released their bombs when they reached their target. The focus on the curtains was really a way to give people something to think about besides their roofs falling in.

There was no such thing as being idle or out of work. Women were either working in the war factories around London or tending to their children at home, while their husbands served in one of the branches of the military. You did what you had to do because it was your duty. And you took comfort in the knowledge that everyone else did likewise. Anyone who didn't follow that protocol would be ignored faster than a speeding rabbit at a dog racetrack after the race was finished.

Our home in Barnes was a self-contained apartment on the ground floor. It had two large bedrooms, one living room, and a kitchen, which had a dangerous gas cooker if it was accidentally extinguished without being lit. There wasn't a bathroom, exactly. Whoever designed the house was thoughtful enough to include a bathtub in the kitchen, and a toilet on the outside of the house. This meant that when I was tall enough and I didn't feel like going outside in the darkness or when it was cold, I peed in the inside sink (something I vigorously denied to my parents, of course). The apartment wasn't very private: we had to be careful when we spoke on the phone since the line was shared with our upstairs neighbor—not an uncommon practice in those days.

It wasn't much, but it was our home. Whenever my father thought that I had grown taller, I would stand against the kitchen door while my father placed a large carving knife on top of my head and scratched the wooden frame. The date would then be added as a record.

We did have a large backyard, the presence of which helped me talk my parents into getting me a dog. I insisted it wasn't just for me, it was for the whole family to enjoy. Enjoy him we did, though I think we were the only ones.

"Pilate" was a crossbreed between a pit bull and a Staffordshire bull terrier. We named him after the vicious Roman Governor Pontius Pilate, and he lived up to his name. Pilate's favorite activity was to get in a fight with another dog and then come home, shake himself, and deposit small specks of blood on the newly wallpapered walls hung by my father.

John, wearing hand-knitted sweater, early 1950s, London.

We knew most of the blood came from the other dog because Pilate would curl himself up and put on a happy face for us, but he was my dog and could do no wrong. We tried not to think about the other dog.

Pilate was a bit of a monster, but we kept him around because, while he was indeed a difficult dog, I was a difficult kid. The dog helped me out enormously: with him to take care of, my whole personality changed from being surly to being good-natured.

My father, the stranger

My father Stephen was an enigma. He spent so much time in the British Navy when I was young that for a while I hardly even knew who he was.

I can remember my father returning home, from the sea, with a large steamer trunk filled with all kinds of goodies from America where he had served part of his service. Inside were can after can of Spam, seamless nylon stockings, for his wife and numerous sisters, and so forth. Most of it wasn't for us.

My father was like that, always thinking of others before himself and his family; consequently, my mother and I were left with whatever no one else wanted, which was practically nothing. He did bring me a Meccano set. But it wasn't long before his family swooped down on the house like vultures and cleaned out nearly everything he had brought.

He even gave away things he'd brought for himself. My father had somehow brought home the ship's bell from *HMS Moorlake*, the ship (now decommissioned) that he had served on. A neighbor once commented on how nice the ship's bell looked in our house. It goes without saying that my neighbor was generously given the bell, and I never saw it again.

I didn't see the touching letter from 1943 that is on page 9 until my mother passed away years later. I was only two when my father wrote it. I hadn't yet seen him and wouldn't see him until the war ended. Officers were given first-class accommodation courtesy of the Royal Navy and the US Government. For my father, it must have been quite a change from wartime London rationing to luxury accommodation and lots of food.

My parents even gave each other unofficial middle names. For my mother, it was "Angelina" after his

"Angel." For my father, it was "John" after me, of course. My parents cleverly managed to slip these names, unnoticed, into their official documents and passports.

Stephen Culnane, St. Paul's Island, Malta, mid-1940s.

My father may have left the British Navy, but he kept the stern and formal attitude that probably served him well as an officer. In addition, he had a temper that resembled a tornado. The slightest thing would set him off, and I set him off frequently.

That isn't to say there wasn't anything there between us. On one occasion, apparently, I deserved a beating. I can't even remember what it was for, but I sat down and

BARBIZON · PLAZA · HOTEL
101 west 58th street · · · central park south · · new york

Room 941.

S/ Culmore ᴵᵀᴿᴬᴺᴷ

5th July 1943

My Darling Mummy,

Well I'm here so far. The first thing I want to do is to wish you a very happy birthday, before leaving England I arranged to have a birthday-card posted to you and also to John to so as to arrive in time for your birthday; I hope that your's arrived OK

The journey over here was uneventful but took rather longer than I thought it would, my first impression of America and for that matter New York was quite different to what I thought it would be; may I say that N.Y. appeared to be much smaller when seen from a distance than it actually is. Upon arrival here I was met at the main station and taken to this Hotel, where I am now staying. Have no fear I am not spending my own money and wondering N at the best hotel. I admit that this hotel is the best in N.Y. but ...

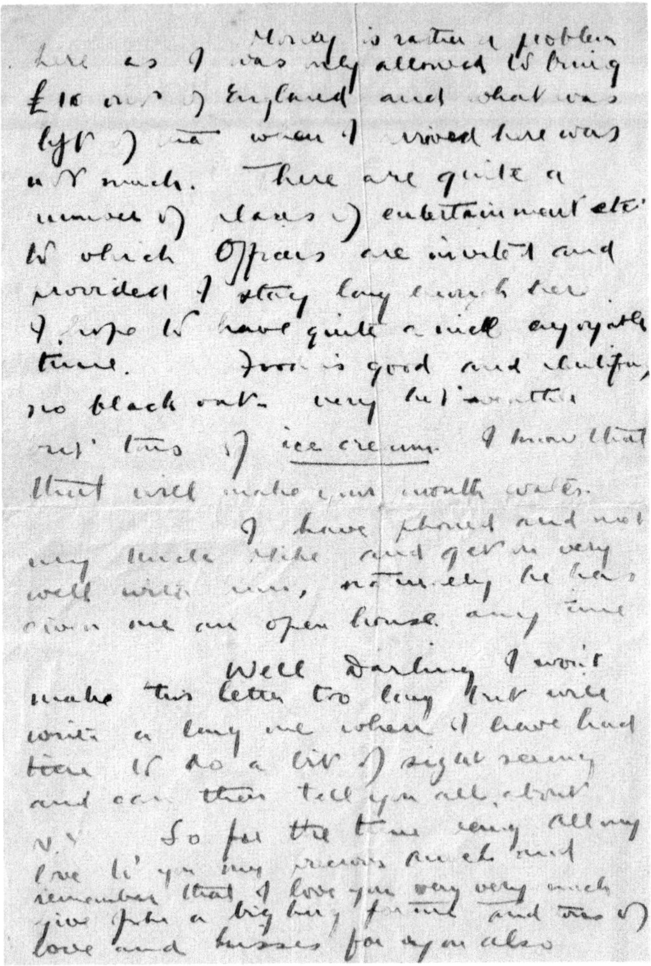

Money is rather a problem here as I was only allowed to bring £10 out of England and what was left of it when I arrived here was not much. There are quite a number of clubs of entertainment etc to which Officers are invited and provided I stay long enough here I hope to have quite a well enjoyable time. Food is good and plentiful, no black out – very hot weather lots of ice cream. I know that that will make your mouth water.

I have phoned and met my Uncle Mike and get on very well with him, naturally he has given me an open house any time.

Well Darling I won't make this letter too long but will write a long one when I have had time to do a bit of sight seeing and can then tell you all about N.Y. So for the time being all my love to you my precious Angel and remember that I love you very very much give John a big hug for me and tons of love and kisses for you also

Letter from Stephen to Helen, New York City, 1943.

Helen Culnane and Lt. Stephen Culnane, Royal Navy.
London 1940s, just married.

calmly said to him, "Dad, can we talk this over?" I must
have connected with an emotional side of him I'd never
seen because he called in my mother to mediate. The
beating never happened, and I lived to be a truculent
kid once more.

He was a heavy smoker who could easily go through
two packs a day. He lost his sense of smell while serving in the navy and compensated with smoking and
snuff. I was the one usually sent to the local store to
buy the snuff; I would not put it in my pocket, because
it stank. I was lucky to avoid getting tangled up in that
unhealthy addiction.

Lt. Stephen Culnane and son John.
London, 1940s.

Helen and Steve Culnane somewhere in Europe. 1960s.
Always wear a tie on vacation.

Stephen Culnane (right) with Dr. G. N.
Shone in New York City, while with Royal Navy, 1940s.

After the war, my father worked as a civil servant in London. His job was to make sure that shops complied with opening and closing hours and that no minors were employed. There were many other things involved also, but that covers the basics. He was regularly approached to overlook infractions and even to accept outright bribes.

He was too disciplined to take the bribes while working for the government. But later, he went into the private sector and became a paid consultant to some people so that they were able to legally circumvent the system. One of these people was Abbas, a middle-aged man from the Middle East. Abbas ran a restaurant and nightclub called "Baghdad House" in Kensington, London, as well as a convenience store next door. My father's consulting work for Abbas eventually became a full-time job.

Abbas knew a lot of powerful people and these people often liked to rent the whole restaurant for the evening. For example, the Rolling Stones would sometimes come and a whole lamb would be cooked for them and their entourage while they watched a belly dancer gyrate her hips to Middle Eastern music.

Eventually, Abbas asked my father to run the whole operation since Abbas made many trips overseas. Usually, Abbas returned in just a few weeks. But on one occasion, he didn't return, and he didn't write or call either. It was as if he'd disappeared off the face of the earth.

With Abbas gone, my father just stepped in and ran the entire operation. He did this for two entire years. When Abbas finally returned, it was very strange: both my father and Abbas acted as if he had only been absent for a few weeks. Abbas thanked my father and gave him a thick heavy envelope.

My father went home and showed the envelope to my mother and me. After much suspense, he finally opened it to reveal £30,000 in cash. At the time, that was a heck of a lot of money; it still is. You had to wonder about someone who could pay out that much cash all at once.

Abbas liked to be the big showman. He kept several extravagant places, including one luxury rental apartment in London, with girlfriend Ms. V. ensconced; one luxury apartment for himself; and one sprawling mansion in the countryside close to London, with a wife, two children, and a dog. I never went there, but my mother did. She said that of all the animals there, she liked the dog most.

One evening I was at Abbas's apartment when someone rapped loudly on the door. Two men stood there in suits and ties and presented their Special Branch identification cards. They wanted to know if Abbas had any weapons in the apartment. They also wanted to know who I was and promptly searched me. I didn't know the details, but this tipped me off that maybe Abbas was in trouble.

That impression was confirmed one evening when my father told me to join him on a short car trip and not to tell my mother. We reached one of the many bridges in London, pulled into a dark side street, and then he showed me a bag full of pistols and ammunition. He told me that Abbas had acquired them because his life was under threat, but now the heat from Special Branch was so great that he had to get rid of the pistols before he got into trouble for possessing them.

My father suggested that I walk with him to the center of the bridge where he would then throw the bag into the icy Thames River; but I said, "No, I'll wait in the car, and you do that." I guess it was a good thing for Abbas that my father did so, because it wasn't long before Special Branch searched all of Abbas's residences, finding nothing, of course.

Abbas came to a bad end though. Much later, I read in a local newspaper that Abbas had been gunned to death in Central London. My father and I speculated on what Abbas had been up to. We could only conclude that he crossed someone in a large business transaction that went wrong.

Some cultures don't believe in legal recourse or bankruptcy—they just permanently eliminate that person with prejudice. My father wasn't too concerned. Despite their years together, Abbas had been a business partner, nothing more.

That was my father: a remote man with a temper, who followed the rules when he had to, but always did what was needed. He wasn't an easy man to live with.

It was clear to my mother and me that my father preferred to be at work than at home. Even meals at home, seated with my father, were rare, because my father managed a restaurant where he could eat whatever he wanted. Judging by his stomach, he did exactly that, which probably led to his early death at age 67. My father didn't believe in going to the doctor for checkups. Doctors were for when you were sick, and not before. Of course, by then it was often too late.

My mother, the trooper

My mother was the real workhorse of the household. She did what she had to do, which included raising me alone while my father was serving in the Navy. And after he returned, she kept on working.

For many years, she was an independent salesperson at Harrods department store in London. She sold a device called "Slender Tone" which, as the name implies, increases muscle and reduces fat. She also sold anything in that department and could make a commission, even though she technically wasn't a Harrods employee. And she could sell anything.

For example, as part of their stock, the store once had a talking pet parrot who had picked up some very nasty words from customers and young staff members. Harrods was eager to sell this bird, but as soon as it opened its mouth, customers ran for the exit. The bird, in disgrace, was put away behind the scenes. A new customer asked if they had any parrots. This wasn't unusual because some of their more eccentric customers expected Harrods to either stock or obtain what they wanted, no matter what the cost, or how strange the request might be.

My mother told the customer that they did, indeed, have a parrot, but the parrot had such a bad mouth that the staff were instructed not to have the bird on display. The intrigued customer asked to see the bird, who promptly let out a torrent of profanities.

The customer got extremely excited and said that he would take the bird immediately. He brought out a check and said, "How much is it?" There was no price tag visible, so my mother quadrupled the price. Not only did my mother get a fat commission, but Harrods also gave her some extra for selling something no one else could or would. My mother was a very shrewd lady.

She was also a very tough lady. At Christmas time 1983, the Irish Republican Army, better known as the IRA, set off a bomb at Harrods that killed six people and caused a million pounds of damage to the store. Three days later, my mother returned to work, business as usual, as if nothing had happened. What else could she do?

Just surviving giving birth to me was an ordeal. My mother had been told, after I was born, that it was unlikely that she would ever have another child. There were medical complications, which later in life caused her to develop painful scar tissue. She eventually had to have a hysterectomy and her ovaries removed.

My mother only told me about the pain, but my father complained that she was now extremely difficult to deal with. My father dealt with this by working from dawn to dusk. The absences were so bad that after more than 12 hours, my mother would tell me to "Take the car and go get your father."

She'd been tough her whole life. Many years later, my mother and I were driving around Barnes when she told me to stop on a side street.

"See that house over there—number two Melville Road?"

"Yes," I answered.

"That's where you were conceived," said my mother matter of factly and proudly. "When the air raid warning

Helen Culnane enjoying the sun somewhere in Europe.

sirens sounded, and your uncle and aunt hid under the stairs, your father and I stayed in the bedroom and produced you."

"You did a good job," I said.

Of course, my mother was a good cook as well. Her *pièce de résistance* was her Sunday roast. This could be either roast beef or roast lamb. If it was a special occasion, then we were treated to half a leg of lamb with all the trimmings. Although I knew that I could eat more, I had to leave room for dessert, which would be equally as good.

All mothers are the best cooks in the world but, if you tell your mother otherwise, you won't get fed. Some weekends we enjoyed going out for an "Indian." There was one Indian restaurant in Earls Court, London, that we particularly liked: The Curry Inn.

After years of going there and getting to know the staff, my mother boldly asked if she could get the recipe for some of the dishes. The staff repeatedly put her off and she left empty-handed, until one day there was a new chef, and he said, "Of course you can have the recipe, I know you'll still come here."

Armed with this recipe, my mother cooked an Indian meal for the first time. It was a disaster. "How was it?" she asked us. I looked at my father, and said, "Dad, you tell Mom how it was." He looked a little embarrassed, squirmed in his chair, and muttered, "It was fine." But she kept at it. After a few more attempts, we were able to proudly tell my mother that her Indian cooking was just as good as the Indian restaurant, and it really was.

My family, in all its glory

We had a lot of family. Since my father had many brothers and sisters, and they lived close by, they were constantly popping in and out to say hello and borrow this or that. His sisters, especially, would rush up to greet me and plant a whopper of a slobbering kiss on my flushed cheeks. But I didn't mind because it was usually followed by a ten-shilling note being placed surreptitiously into my hot little hands. Later, my parents would ask me how much I had been given, as if to see what the aunt thought I was worth. When I reached my teenage years, all the hugs, kisses, and money stopped. It made me wonder why they'd ever done it.

Although I remained close with many of my nearby aunts and uncles, I never learned much about my great-grandparents' side of the family on my father's side, and my father wasn't talking. Despite being part of a large family, he never spoke about them or produced any photographs, which I thought was strange, to say the least.

I only saw one family photograph many years later that one of my aunts had managed to save. It showed my grandfather at his wedding with his young bride. Since my grandparents died in their fifties, I never had the opportunity to know them, and to this day I'm still trying to find out more about them and my great-grandparents and who their parents were. It's all still a mystery that no one bothered to document or pass down the story.

There was one relative I did get to spend a good amount of time with: my Aunt Jo on my father's side, who lived in an old Victorian house nearby in Barnes. (Everyone in the Culnane family lived in Barnes, but I don't know why.) In those days, Barnes was a working-class neighborhood populated with large houses. Many of them were five-bedroom houses, being shared by more people than bedrooms. Census records indicate that in the early 1900s six or eight in a family household wasn't uncommon.

When a phone call came from my Aunt Jo, I always knew that I was in for a long conversation coupled with copious amounts of sherry. (See, I told you the sherry was a good way to start stories flowing.) Jo loved to tell me about my connections to long-forgotten relatives. I didn't always know all the people involved, but dutifully wrote everything down on a large chart in the hope that it made sense later. No one else seemed interested, so I eventually took it upon myself to update a family tree based upon my cousin Mike's previous extensive genealogical research.

I always used to admire an old French carriage clock sitting on my aunt's antique mantelpiece. Aunt Jo eventually gave me the clock, which I have to this day. It doesn't work, but it's the only thing remaining of her possessions. Cousin Mike provided the foundation, and gradually over the years, others became interested in their Culnane family history.

I have to wonder if, in a hundred years, any remaining Culnanes will even know or care who their ancestors were. My Aunt Jo was also very interested in talking about the past. Aunt Jo liked to tell the story

about the Culnanes's connection to the Cullinan diamond found in South Africa in 1905. But I don't think
the Culnanes had any claim to that gigantic gemstone,
supposedly, the largest ever found. Had there been, the
media would surely have hunted them down. So far, no
one has called.

Aunt Jo once told my mother, "You will remember
me when I'm under the floorboards." My mother and
I thought that perhaps Aunt Jo would remember my
mother in her will. My mother said, "Be nice to your
Aunt Jo, she's going to remember us."

When Aunt Jo eventually died about thirty years
later, in 1984, we discovered that my mother had been
left the princely sum of £250, which was worth consid-
erably less than it had been in the 1950s. If my aunt Jo
had left my mother a percentage of the estate, instead of
a fixed amount, then my mother would have been sitting on a goldmine that she would not easily forget. The
£250 was quickly spent, but the memories my mother
and I had of Aunt Jo were not so quick to evaporate.
She was a rare exception though. For the most part,
despite the large Culnane presence in Barnes, "family"
meant my parents and me, but mostly my mother.

From the little tidbits that were extracted (like pull-
ing teeth) from my father, I gathered that life in that
large family was tough and strict. Hand-me-downs
were passed from brother to brother and sister to sister
without any quibbles. The younger siblings would sit
around peeling potatoes and vegetables in large buckets
until they were given their next task. I'm quite sure that

the kids were punished whenever they failed to complete a task. Not once did I ever hear my father praise his parents.

They weren't a wealthy family, but they had what they needed; census records show my grandparents ran a butcher and greengrocer shop. When my grandmother Mary Agnes died, her estate was worth less than £392 (about £30,000 in today's money). Her husband Charles died a year later. Many of my father's siblings were later buried in paupers' graves, impossible to locate with any exactitude decades later.

Yet, somehow, the family erected a very elaborate and expensive gravestone for Mary Agnes and Charles. It just didn't make sense to me because my father never went there. I only discovered the gravestone many years later when I was researching my family history. While being left £392 was a considerable amount of money in the 1930s, the family still felt this marker was unimportant. Most likely the elaborate gravestone was stipulated in their wills.

What that says to me is this: your parents are an important part of your story, even if you didn't like the way you were brought up. Perhaps, later, the siblings came to appreciate their parents more. Maybe they didn't all feel the way my father did. Who knows? Unfortunately, their stories went to their graves for eternity.

Lesson 1: The sadistic nuns of Bridport

After the war, there was a lot of celebration and many people went back to their normal lives. It turned out that normal life with me at home was a little more than my parents were ready to deal with. Also, they probably needed more time to themselves after the long war.

They decided that it would be a good idea to send me far away at the age of eight to a boarding school run by Catholic nuns. It had been good enough for several of my uncles, so it would be good enough for me. In any event, I had no choice.

That's how I became kitted out in a maroon blazer, cap, and shorts. It didn't look too bad, so I went along with it without creating a tantrum, which I was well known for. How awful could this be—a train ride to Bridport, Dorset, with black smoke billowing through the windows, an egg and cheese sandwich, which smelled of sulfur, and an army of smiling nuns who couldn't wait to get their evil hands on me and all the other innocent boys?

My first introduction to the Visitation Convent, Bridport, Dorset involved lining up naked with all the other new boys. We were then given a sponge bath and our hair was disinfected for lice in case we had any. I didn't have any then, but I sure did soon. After a few days, I found them crawling around as if they owned my body; worse, they seemed to demand that I scratch them to keep them awake so that they could bite me more.

I thought at least that we'd get some good food— after all, we were in the countryside right next to cows, sheep, and chickens. I could also see rows of apple, plum and pear trees that made my mouth water. After years in wartime and post-war London, where ration books were the rule, it seemed like I'd come to a land of plenty.

But none of this good country food was for me or the other boys. All of it was for the nuns to eat or sell. It certainly wasn't for the boys under their care. I realized how well the nuns ate while casually entering their restricted refectory. Immediately my nostrils inhaled wafts of bacon, something I vaguely remembered from much earlier as a child. I saw real eggs and lots of fruit and wondered why I didn't get any of that.

Since we all ate together, the nuns disallowed any talking while we were eating. The nuns preferred to eat their meals in silence rather than listen to numerous young boys jabbering away. If you chose to disobey this rule, then you knew that punishment would be meted out to the miscreants. It was easy for me to keep my mouth shut and avoid becoming a miscreant because I was too busy eating the disgusting sparse food within a limited time frame.

Although the war had ended, rationing was still in effect. Each boy had his own ration book issued to him— which the nuns promptly used for their own benefit.

Some of the boys talked about why we weren't getting any of this good stuff; so, we decided to take some for ourselves. We found long branches and string and a small weight, much like a fishing pole, and then we went fishing for fruit, over the fence that separated us from the orchard.

We collected so much that it was more than we could eat; we gave some away to other boys. That was our mistake because it led to our discovery. As soon as the nuns found out about our exploits, we were summoned into the office of the Mother Superior one by one. We knew that this visit was not to ask how we were getting along.

Mother Superior reached into a big cupboard and handed what was in there to another nun. Mother Superior told me to bend over. I briefly saw the well-worn bamboo cane just before I felt the excruciating searing pain and let out a howl like a wild animal. I lost count, but I think it was about five strokes. I was then asked if I intended to repeat what I had done. Of course, I said no. It was then that I realized that my young life was going to be hell, and this was only the beginning.

As I received more canings, I eventually became numb to the pain. However, this advantage was not something I was going to share with the nuns. I kept up the shrieks and howls to make sure they felt satisfied with the way they handled the caning and me. To this day, I'm unable to recall what I did to deserve those beatings. After all, what could an eight-year-old boy do to warrant such physical abuse?

Many children go on to learn that beating someone, whether it be a child or a weaker spouse, gets results. This pattern then often trickles down through the generations and becomes the norm. I, fortunately, never followed this pattern of behavior. But it was a lousy way to spend my school years.

Because of the proximity of the boys and the layout of the school, boys were often catching all kinds of illnesses. Mild colds warranted a dose of cough medicine so strong and unpleasant that you would never complain again about having a cough or cold.

Beatings were only for big sins. For most minor infractions, the nuns would swipe your tongue with a revolting piece of black rock. This had the effect of making you want to throw up. In class, while they were teaching multiplication tables, if you kept making mistakes, they would rap your knuckles with a heavy wooden ruler until you gave the correct answer.

Punishment: that was the intent of the nuns. Nothing less, nothing more.

Consequently, I learned at an early age not to make mistakes. My parents always admired the letter-perfect letters I wrote home from school, but they never knew the price I paid, and I never told them. I still have some of those letters my mother kept. The letters were, of course, censored by the nuns, so I could only say good things about my time at the Visitation Convent.

Getting fed by the nuns wasn't a problem. It's just that the food presented was not something usually eaten by animals, let alone children. The food we were given was mostly waste products such as offal and tripe. The bread was often stale and given to the boys, rather than the nuns so that nothing was wasted. We might have been young naïve boys, but we knew that the bread had to have been fresh at some point, and that point was when it entered the stomachs of the nuns long before we saw it.

When it came to the quality and quantity of the food, the nuns had the pick of the crop. Considering that the nuns' convent was practically self-sufficient with their own dairy and crop farms, the nuns lacked for nothing. It was a different story for the boys. Chiefly waste and whatever the nuns couldn't or wouldn't eat was given to the boys. This was especially true with products that had gone off or were stale. To the boys, this was the norm.

None of this could be told to our parents because the weekly letters sent home were scripted to paint a happy child, in a happy place with caring and happy nuns.

A typical breakfast consisted of powdered eggs and dark moldy bread. Dinner, usually called supper, was often liver, black sausage, and spaghetti every day. Some of the bowls used to deliver the food were also used as vomit buckets when one of the boys was sick. Even today, I cannot eat spaghetti—thinking about it makes me gag.

Boys being boys, we tried other ways to supplement our diet. Once, some of the boys got hold of mustard and cress seeds, and we planted them in blotting paper taken from our desks. We laid them in the drain gutters of the building, so the seeds got a constant drip of water. This went on for ages until we got caught.

We knew what the consequences would be, but it was worth it to eat fresh vegetables we had grown ourselves—not to mention the look of incredulity on the faces of the nuns. Some boys were slow learners.

They dipped the blotting paper into the blue inkwells, wrapping them with rubber bands, and slung them at the nuns when their backs were turned. I never did this because the punishment, if caught, was worse than any eight-year-old boy could imagine.

Nobody mentioned, to us boys, that we were in the middle of the Jurassic Coastal area, interestingly, now a UNESCO World Heritage Site. But we could see for ourselves that there was something special and different about the area. Boys were constantly finding fossils, and the race was on to see who could find the best fossil.

Each Sunday, all the boys would be taken on walks to West Bay. The only difference between us and dogs being taken for walks is that we didn't have physical leashes on us, only mental restraints. Along the way, we passed clusters of horse chestnut trees and tried to gather up conkers for games to be played later, but the nuns weren't having any of that and would make us keep up with the group. After about three miles, we were glad to arrive at the sandstone cliffs of West Bay, Dorset.

We immediately put our sore feet into the icy water to cool them off. Then the nuns brought us lemonade powder mixed with pure spring water from the cliffs, and we drank until we could drink no more. We then searched for periwinkle snails among the rocks and, using a safety-pin, pulled out the meat inside, and ate them raw. The nuns just sat and watched us.

Fortunately, the return trip was on a bus. After many walks, the leather on our shoes invariably wore out and the nails fastening the leather penetrated the inner sole resulting in sore bloody feet. The nuns had seen this all before and daubed our feet with tincture of iodine. The shoes were then hammered until the nails no longer protruded. One of the boys developed a nasty foot infection for which the nuns applied a hot mustard compress. Being curious boys, we watched as the pus gradually decreased until he completely recovered.

While the nuns didn't feel it was necessary to give us toys to play with or books to read, other than prayer books, to occupy our young and fertile minds, they did organize games for us to play. The egg-and-spoon race and the potato sack race were favorites for the boys, even if some of the boys did scrape their knees in the process. Running around a pole at the end of a rope and suddenly letting go, made the boys dizzy and flying off in all directions, much to the amusement of the nuns who laughed uncontrollably like hyenas. We didn't find it so funny as we behaved like drunken sailors solely for their amusement.

It wasn't all caning and punishment—day trips to local resorts such as Swanage and Lyme Regis, Dorset, were a special treat with afternoon teas given to the exuberant boys.

My time at the convent school did teach me a few valuable lessons. I learned that, no matter how harsh the circumstances, people will find a way to get by, even kids. For example, once I was surprised to see a group of boys with their ears glued to the metal railings of the bed. As I got closer, I could hear music and voices coming from a wire wrapped around the frame of the bed.

They had a crystal radio to listen to, though they only used it at night when the nuns were sleeping. I was confused, because this wire contraption didn't look much like the large wooden-boxed radio my parents had at home. But it was neat. That said, I didn't shed any tears when my time with the nuns was done.

When this whole show was over, I was released back to my parents, much like a prisoner. I told them about what went on there, but they didn't believe a word I said. They thought I made it up. Gradually, word got out through other boys and their parents, that what I had been saying all along was truthful. It seemed kind of late to me, though.

Lesson 2: The cruel cadets and bully boys of Holbrook

After my return from the convent school, I think my father believed that I still needed more structure and discipline. Talk of Military School became a common topic of discussion around the dinner table. This time, I was older, so was included in the conversation and decision-making. Even so, my parents convinced me that the Royal Hospital School in Suffolk would be a good choice for me.

It wasn't a hospital school in the sense of where you learn medical skills, but a large naval training center. It was also a place where defiant boys were usually sent for correction, but I didn't know that. So, once again, I found myself on a train, headed in a different direction, to a different place of suffering.

I thought that I had learned quite a bit from the nuns about discipline and punishment; unfortunately, I didn't realize how much more there was to learn.

The whole idea of a naval training center for boys is to break them down physically and mentally, and then rebuild with them values, skills, discipline, and a host of other attributes to enable them to live useful lives; some of them might even join the Navy. The nuns' punishment was just mean-spirited, a way to keep rambunctious boys under control.

This punishment was systematic. While the food was undeniably better at the military school, the amount of bullying from the older and more senior-ranking boys, was intense to the point of being cruel, unbearable, immoral, and downright illegal. I realized that the bullying was all part of the plan to "man you up," but they went too far on a ten-year-old boy.

I'm not sure if I believe in the supernatural, but, having said that, an incident occurred that made me seriously question my beliefs. I was sitting in the crowded dining hall of the Royal Hospital School and mentioned to a fellow diner that the glass I was holding would break. I don't know why I said this, but the glass broke into many small pieces. There was not one person in the school, including the headmaster, who did not hear about this. I never came to understand the meaning of the glass breaking after I said that it would.

Swimming was always an important activity at the Naval School. It was more than important; it was mandatory to know how to swim. Several times a week, a group of the boys would strip off naked and swim laps of the pool under the overly watchful eye of the male adult teachers. If we felt particularly adventurous, some of the boys would swing on the trapeze and make Tarzan moves and sounds. I didn't do that because if you were unfortunate enough to be left stranded in the middle, you were expected to drop into the pool. I wasn't sure whether the pool was deep enough at that point, but I had no intention of finding out.

The Naval school was not my first introduction to weapons, since my mother's family were all farmers and had all kinds of weapons, mostly shotguns, which I got to handle but not shoot, except for the airguns. But being a military school, sooner or later weapons would be fired.

So, I learned as much as a ten-year-old could about rifles and bayonets. I discovered that not only did I love it, but I was also good at shooting rifles accurately despite the heavy recoil. This was something that would carry through into my civilian marksmanship as well as my military marksmanship. I was only twenty-one when I got my first trophy cup. Naively, I asked when I could take this large trophy cup home, but they said I would only get to have my name inscribed on it and have my photograph taken.

Sports have always played an important role in bringing up young boys. Holbrook Military School was no exception. At Holbrook, boxing was one of the sports. Sometimes, boxing matches were exhibited to the whole school. Boxing, I soon found out, is a lot more entertaining to watch than to experience.

Once, while I was sitting in the bleachers with all the other boys and expecting to be entertained, my name was called, and I was taken to a side room where boxing gloves were fitted to my, by now, trembling hands. Then I was led to the ring like a gladiator being fed to the lions. It was all over in minutes and I left the ring with a bloody nose amid cheering from the boys and staff. I never found out if they were cheering for me or my much older opponent.

Once again, I was taken advantage of, this time for the amusement of others. Even though I was only ten years old, something inside of me told me to remain strong in body, mind, and spirit. I knew that although I might be beaten physically, my mind would never be beaten.

One of the senior boys, who was directly in charge of me and five years older than me, started taking me to a remote changing area seldom used. There he sexually abused me and forced me to perform sexual acts on him. At first, I resisted, and he repeatedly beat me, telling me that he was my senior and I had to obey him. This went on for some time and I just complied. What else could I do? I already knew people didn't believe you when you reported horrible things that happened.

This went on until one very cold day, we were marching to the mess hall and I started shivering uncontrollably, fainted, and dropped to the ground. I woke up in the infirmary not knowing what happened. The doctor was asking me why I had so much bruising on my back, but I couldn't tell him because I didn't know I had it. Then they brought in a professional to interview me and get the whole story. Then the truth came out. It wasn't pretty.

After a few hours, they pieced together what had happened. The school expelled the older boy, who probably lost a promising career in the Navy, and sent me home to London. That was it. In those days, things like that were just swept under the rug. But the psychological bruises remained long after the physical ones were gone.

Lesson 3: Don't drink the sacramental wine

Now, I was back home again, a problem child who was a veteran of not one but two boarding schools. They

Choirboy, Westminster Cathedral Choir School, 1954.

were supposed to give me discipline and structure, but instead I came home with bruises and bad memories.

What were my parents going to do with me next? My mother's next idea was quite different. She suggested that I audition for Westminster Cathedral Choir. Her own singing voice was good, and she saw some musical potential in me. Other than the fees, the main requirements were that you had an excellent voice, were of the right age, and were Catholic.

For reasons I will never understand, I passed the audition to the Choir School with flying colors. This was a dream come true. Instead of beatings from sadistic nuns and worse from even more sadistic military cadets, I learned how to sing in a world-class choir and how to read music. I even made a little pocket money, ten shillings at a time, from singing recordings and film scores, which I spent on necessities like vanilla fudge straight out of the cookie jar from a local candy shop. I had finally found something I was good at and enjoyed. Most of all, I was happy, even if I was homesick. To make things even better, the food was more than sufficient. Sometimes—not wanting to seem greedy—I'd wait until the other boys had left and finish off the scones, butter, and jam that I craved so much.

Our big day came when rationing was lifted for candy and sugar-related products in 1953. All the children in London and elsewhere rushed to the candy stores and completely cleaned them out. Row after row of large empty candy jars was all that remained for those not quick enough to get there first.

Soccer Team, Westminster Cathedral Choir School, 1953.
John is in the middle row, second from the right. Nicolas Kynaston,
organist, is in the middle row, first from the right.

Being in a Catholic Cathedral Choir meant that, as a matter of course, I sang in English, Latin, Greek, French and Italian. I quickly developed a flair for foreign languages, as well as those taught at the Choir School. As for other subjects I didn't like, my teachers said I was lazy, and could do more.

For some reason, my mother kept those reports and I still have some of them. I think that many parents with underperforming students secretly hope that they can rub their teachers' noses in their child's future successes.

Choir School was great, but there's a drawback: it only lasts until your voice breaks, usually around thirteen. Then, the boys transition from choir singers to altar boys who get to serve at mass everyday, and sometimes for the foreign priests who are obliged to say mass.

Imagine my delight when I found out that these priests were told to tip the altar boys. I easily made five to ten shillings per day. In addition, I got to prepare the South African sacramental wine for the mass each day. It was only natural that I should periodically try a sip of this wine, before it was blessed, of course. I wasn't going to push my luck and get excommunicated for drinking blessed wine.

The Cathedral Choir School knew that some boys would like a drink now and then because, occasionally, we were treated to a glass of Stones Ginger Wine—which I never refused. It was a treat, but it also had the effect of calming the more disruptive boys, of which I was one. This was one of my earliest experiences with alcohol. It sure wouldn't be my last.

It wasn't all altar boy tips and ginger wine, though. This school punished students too. I still received caning or remedial treatment, though not as frequently as I had experienced with the nuns. Here, the caning was more a way of exercising authority, rather than for any minor transgressions.

For example, if you didn't respond quickly enough with the right answer, the cane might appear. You had to assume that the cane would appear at any time, so, it was in your interest to pay attention and learn; obviously, that was something that I didn't always do.

The main highlight of being in the Westminster Cathedral Choir School was being taught music by choirmaster Sir George Malcolm and organist Maxwell Fernie. Their knowledge of music was unparalleled, as well as their desire for others to learn—no matter how much time it took. It is fair to say that Mr. Malcolm was worshipped by the boys but disliked by the administration of the cathedral for his unorthodox teaching methods, not to mention his drinking.

Mr. Malcolm, as he was known then, liked his alcohol and sometimes it showed. For one afternoon service, Mr. Malcolm took his usual place at the apse end of the cathedral, raised his baton to conduct, and it went flying, much to the amusement of the choristers. We didn't care. We loved him, and he loved us.

Drinking wasn't limited to the choirmaster. Many of the adult bass and baritone members of the choir liked to indulge also. Since they sat right behind us, we could smell their beer breaths. Perhaps it made their voices richer. While they sat waiting for their time to sing, they often whittled away with a penknife on a piece of hardwood, much like the old fishermen on boats far away with too much time on their hands. In hindsight, all the drinking by Mr. Malcolm and the other choir members doesn't seem as funny. But at the time, it didn't bother me. What did I know? I was just a kid.

At the Cathedral Choir School, we were once given the task of learning a poem for an assignment. As it happened, my parents both enjoyed poetry and, together, learned long poems, which they would often recite for my enjoyment. They encouraged me to learn some of them too. Their favorite was "Elegy Written in a Country Churchyard," by Thomas Gray. Consequently, I was more than ready for this task.

When my turn came to recite a poem, I very calmly recited five stanzas in a row. I was about to continue, when the teacher said, "Thank you, John, that will be all." The teacher and students just stared at me in silence while I maintained my look of smugness. After that, I was never asked to recite any more poetry.

My voice had broken, and puberty was beckoning. My time at the choir school was coming to an end when it all came crashing down. I was called into the office of Headmaster Father Thomas Kilcoyne. He got right down to business and asked me, why I had written something bad on the bathroom walls. When I explained that I didn't know anything about it, or even what the words meant, he simply said that I had until 4:00 p.m. that day to admit it and all would be forgiven, or my father would be called and I would be expelled.

Of course, I chose to admit it even though I hadn't the slightest idea what the word was that appeared on the wall. Four o'clock arrived and my father was waiting in Father Kilcoyne's office. I was shocked. I had been tricked: I'd confessed to something I hadn't done and had been expelled for it despite the headmaster's promise. I never did understand why this happened. The lesson I took away from that was that priests and nuns lied and could not be trusted.

Lesson 4: Morden Technical and discovering girls

And so, it came about that I was to enter yet another school. I couldn't wait to be an adult so I could put all this behind me and start living my life like everyone else. However, the rules were clear: you had to finish school. Otherwise, you were likely to end up on the slag heap of layabouts or slackers. My parents and I were determined to see my education through.

The next school, or rather institution, was Morden Technical School in South London. This seemed to be where all the rejects ended up, so I instantly fit in. Here, along with all the usual academic subjects, we received training in wood and metal crafts. For those deemed unfit to use their brains, this was the place where your hands would define you. I loved it. No more beating or bullying or being screamed at. Just you, a chisel, a plane and a piece of wood. I was in heaven.

I discovered two things at Morden. The first was that I loved to plan and make things. I learned how to craft wood and metal using my hands as well as machines. I was shown how to create a blueprint for wood or metal production. The sky was the limit, I could make anything as far as I was concerned. What this did was occupy my mind and my body in a way that was not boring. I became less disruptive and more attentive because I enjoyed what I was doing.

The second thing I discovered was girls. By now I was a teenager with hormones raging through me every moment of every day. I wasn't exactly sure what was going on in my body, but whatever it was, I liked it.

It transformed my vision; instead of seeing a pimply young girl with unkempt hair, I saw a goddess worthy of my attention.

Of course, neither my parents nor my teachers, in all this time and all these different schools, had bothered to teach me about the facts of life. I had to learn about it on the streets, and what I learned wasn't always accurate. I once entered a communal toilet and noticed what I thought was a bloody rag on the floor, I immediately rushed out and told an adult that there had been an accident. I guess geometry and multiplication were essential subjects to learn, but the facts of life were apparently unimportant.

My journey to school involved several train changes and took about an hour. In those days, schools were segregated between boys and girls, but we did get to link up with the girls on the train journeys. One particular girl lived almost next to me in Barnes, so I escorted her safely from the train station to an intersection close to her house. That was as close to her as I was going to get, regrettably.

When I dropped her off each time, "JC" gave me such an incandescent smile, that I thought I had died and gone to heaven. I was given the privilege of carrying her satchel of heavy books. I would have gone to school seven days a week just for that. I thought, subconsciously, that she deliberately loaded up her satchel with heavy books so that I would feel obligated to carry them.

My parents thought it might be a good idea to meet me on my way back from the train station one time.

I didn't know what to say, as I was carrying JC's satchel. After that, my parents casually teased me: "John, how is your little friend?" John's got himself a girlfriend, he's fair game.

Unfortunately for me, I didn't really have a girlfriend. JC had other suitors at her beck and call who would meet her at the train station and occasionally deprive me of my job carrying her satchel and ensuring her safety. What's worse, she rewarded them in a way she never did me. Sometimes she would sneak off with these other boys and she would tell me later that they kissed. How I wished that was me and not them. I should have realized that if she had wanted to be with me, she would have been.

Once she told me, teasingly, that she was going to apply a moisturizing cream to her legs; I gallantly offered to do that for her. She then told me that she was going to allow one of the other boys to do that. It was disappointing, but I soldiered on. At that point, I believed I was in love because the smile I received when she reached home was so massive that it could not be anything but love for her also; she was light years ahead of me in maturity, even though we were both about 15. That girl could surely unlock doors without keys.

I eventually realized that I was being manipulated, but I didn't care. I was a very naïve young boy with much to learn in the many years ahead. My first love turned out to be a tease, and no more than a mirage in the desert of dreams—poor John.

Lesson 5: Girls who liked to drink, smoke and dance

Weekends were often spent at dances at the Castle Hotel, Richmond. One of my friends and I would find partners from the crowd and shuffle clumsily around a dance floor. We preferred the slow songs which involved dancing cheek to cheek, or close body contact with a girl who didn't mind having her feet stepped on.

If the girl who didn't mind having her feet stepped on was interested, you would find a table and buy her a drink; otherwise, she would be dropped like a hot potato! She would then pull out a cigarette and expect you to light it for her. This lighting of the cigarette was a whole ritual and separated the men from the boys. Since I was a nonsmoker, the thought of kissing a girl who smoked was not high on my agenda. But if the girl was hot enough, I was willing to have my mind changed; and I found my mind being changed frequently.

This sometimes led to dates for dinner, dancing, or movies, but not all at the same time as it was too expensive. Usually, I went to movies. It didn't matter what the movie was about because I wasn't going to watch it anyway. But I would tell the girl that a really good movie was playing at the Odeon or whatever cinema it happened to be and meet her there at seven o'clock. They didn't all start at seven, but I didn't care. If we got there too late, I would just say, "They must have changed the times."

Most of the time, she didn't care either because it wasn't long before our tongues were furiously exploring each other. Sometimes, if it was my lucky night, she wore a skirt instead of the usual slacks, accompanied by a big smile; I took this to be all part of my extracurricular education, and eagerly went along with it. I went to a lot of movies for which I can neither remember the name, the actors, or what it was about.

Money was tight in those days, so wining and dining had to be viewed as an investment in my future. If I spent all my money on girls who didn't work out, there would be none left to spend on girls with potential. It was a little like going to the racetrack: if you didn't bet, you couldn't win. Every first date was a gamble and they didn't all pay off.

Afterwards, sometimes my parents would ask me what movie I saw. And I would ask, "How did you know I went to a movie?" My mother, usually, said, "I can smell the cigarette smoke on your clothes." Since I didn't smoke, this was indeed a clue.

Even the painted ceilings of the movie theaters were stained yellow from so much cigarette smoke. I hated that my parents wanted to know every detail of my life, but there wasn't much I could do about it other than avoid girls who smoked. And there were too many pretty girls who smoked for me to do that.

When I was attending school, a lot of bad behavior went on in the toilets. I tried to avoid them whenever possible, but eventually, I had to go. There were students puffing away on cigarettes, choking, and pretending to enjoy them. Once, two boys disappeared into one of the cubicles and did things in there that everyone in the school seemed to know and gossip about; but I had no interest in such things. If I wanted to go into a cubicle with someone else, it certainly wouldn't be with a boy, it would be with a girl. However, being a boys-only school, that wasn't going to happen.

I did try one puff of a cigarette, but I choked on it. To me, it was like sticking my head up a chimney and inhaling. I never again wanted to repeat that disgusting process for any type of addictive drug whether it be cigarettes or marijuana. Alcohol was to be a different kettle of fish though. Maybe if alcohol were just as disgusting as cigarettes, I could have avoided problems later on.

The last lesson: What do I want to be when I grow up?

Once I had finally finished with school, it was time for my life to begin in earnest. I had to decide, as an adult, what I wanted to do. My education hadn't exactly trained me for a specific career. I thought about what I knew most about and enjoyed. I had liked being in the choir, although I didn't want to play an instrument or sing for a job. I had liked creating things with my hands. I had also learned to like pipe organ music and often listened to it at the cathedral. When I put all this together, I realized that pipe organ building seemed to combine all the things I wanted.

So, I went to London for an interview with Henry Willis & Sons, pipe organ builders. I was hired and immediately immersed in the tuning side of the business.

This was fine for me, because I was able to learn all the keyboard notes while traveling around the major London churches that had huge pipe organs. Eventually, they let me loose in the manufacturing side of things.

By this time, I had matured more and was causing fewer problems for people. The tantrums of my youth were a thing of the past; for the first time, I was in control of my environment. I blended in more. I felt comfortable in my own skin. For a while, at least, I was able to live, instead of just survive.

PART 2

America

fter a few years, though, I got restless: I wanted something different. Despite the stability I'd found, a lot of London and the surroundings held very mixed memories for me. I wanted something exciting that involved traveling. I hadn't traveled outside of Europe before. My impressions of the outside world were still few and far between—it was a place you disappeared to and returned with exotic things, like my father did when he served in the Navy. It was time, I thought, for me to have my own adventure.

Crossing the pond without getting my feet wet

As it happened, I had a place to go: The United States. My Uncle Mick lived in Queens, New York, and he agreed to put me up upon my arrival. My first encounter with a long-distance airline involved a turboprop plane with a stopover in Iceland. The weather was extremely turbulent, and I arrived in New York feeling as if I was constantly being dropped down an elevator shaft. It was a relief to step off the plane, onto a new land, and into a new chapter of my life.

Uncle Mick, Aunt Mary, and Cousin Tony lived in the neighborhood of Rego Park in Queens, New York. They were very welcoming and made me feel right at home. Uncle Mick worked for a cargo vessel company that transported bananas from Callao, Peru, to the Port of New York.

The ship had a few cabins aboard for passengers, and Uncle Mick acted as a purser aboard the ship. He invited me to the ship, one time, where he thrust a bundle of cigarette cartons under my jacket and told me to disembark. I only realized later that I had, unwittingly, broken US customs law with a little bit of smuggling.

I liked Americans. In those days, Americans had always been easy to pick out in the crowd back home because of the cut of their clothes and the ubiquitous button-down shirt collars the men wore. And that was apart from their loud voices and their brash behavior worldwide.

Eventually, fashion melted into one giant pot of blue jean sameness, and other nationalities overtook the Americans in their fondness for splashing money around and raising hell. But at the time, America was something else, maybe even hippie-dippy heaven.

After a few months of craning my neck looking at New York skyscrapers and eating hot dogs and sauerkraut, I was ready to move on. This time I found my way to Los Angeles, California, clear on the other side of the country. I found myself learning a whole new set of words and phrases; compared to what I'd heard in New

York and London, Californian was almost like a new language. But the people were friendly and nice, the weather was good, and it was on the Pacific coast. Now all I needed was a job.

Learning the new language!

When I got to Los Angeles and it became clear that I planned to stick around in the country for a while, I had to get permission to stay. I was lucky: each country and region was given a quota, and the UK was high on the list compared to someone from a lesser-known region with a different language. Consequently, because of my good looks (not really) and proficiency in English, I was immediately given a green card to maintain my stay in the US. But this came with a catch: I was required to register for the draft. No, not the NFL draft—the US armed forces draft. I hadn't really been paying too much attention to the political situation around the world, but Vietnam was high on the political agenda at the time, and the US Army was going to need a lot more boots on the ground. I didn't think much about this when I got my green card, but it sure became an issue later.

I got a job in a local department store, Robinson's, on Grand Avenue, close to where I lived at the Embassy Hotel. It was all very convenient: the hotel was $48 per month, and I was making about $150 per month at the store. This gave me a nice amount of pocket money to enjoy myself in sunny Southern California. I soon realized, though, that it wasn't all sunshine in Los Angeles. On one hot summer day in early August 1965, I had just left work when I noticed a large crowd watching a television in the shop window. They didn't look like the sports crowd I normally saw.

As I got closer, the crowd continued to grow. Then I saw the images of the Watts riots, which were taking place not far from where I was standing. Young men with bloodied faces, overturned cars, and buildings being set alight. I continued to watch since there was no TV in my room at the Embassy Hotel, despite its grand name. It was alarming to see. Right next to the store was a huge billboard with a sign: "WHY WALK AROUND HALF DEAD WHEN WE CAN BURY YOU FOR $295." Nice, I had to walk past that every day and think I was only worth $295. With scenes of violence from the riots fresh in my mind, it was an unpleasant thought.

When "Uncle Sam" speaks, you listen

However, I came to realize that I was worth much more alive to the US Armed Forces. A letter arrived that I had to sign for. It looked especially important, and it was. Inside was a personal letter from the President of the United States, or so it seemed. It stated, "Greetings, John Culnane! You are hereby informed that you are to report for induction into the US Armed Forces on 12 October 1965." That was only in a few weeks. I had managed to work for about six months; now I had just a short time left before I would belong to the US Government.

Whatever they wanted to do with me, they could and would. Wartime America had caught up with me.

American citizens were fleeing to Canada in droves to avoid the draft. I had only just arrived in the US. I knew that if I left now, I would never be readmitted. I came to the US for adventure, and I liked it there. I didn't want to leave. I decided that I would follow through, whatever happened.

"Yes, Sir"

Now I was in the US Army with what seemed like a truckload of spare uniforms, including fatigues, summer dress khaki uniforms, and even a winter dress green uniform. And it was all crammed into a duffel bag almost my size and weight. I looked surprisingly good in the uniform, and they must have realized that because they took my photograph. Of course, they took everyone else's photo for their ID card also. So maybe I didn't look as good as I thought.

Next, we had our hair cut practically to the bone. Some of the men asked for their hair to be cut in a certain style, but we all emerged the same, looking like prisoners being prepared for execution. Our fingers were pricked, and blood was taken to determine our blood type. We were then asked our religion, and that was it. We were now part of one big happy family: The US Army.

Custom dog tags were made for each of us so that if we got killed in action, the officer could simply break off one of the tags from the body, and everyone would know with certainty the ID of that body. When it came to corpse identification, the US Army had you covered.

To make things better, you had $2 deducted from your paycheck each month for a $10,000 life insurance policy, which covered you whether you died falling down a manhole or got blown to bits in a place in Asia you had never heard of.

Of course, you wouldn't receive the money yourself because you would be dead. But you could rest easy knowing that your loved ones would finally be able to make a down payment on a house that they always wanted but could never afford; you just wouldn't be in it.

We all assembled in a large hall with our new uniforms and closely cropped hair. An officer addressed us and laid out some basic rules with which we were

SGT. John P. Culnane
Fort Benning, Georgia, 1966.

SGT. John P. Culnane, London, 1966.

expected to follow without question. The first one involved saluting officers every time you met them. Someone raised their hand to ask a question—that was one of the rules, raising your hand.

"Sir, how do we know if that person is an officer?" said the new recruit.

"If he's not smiling, he's an officer," said the officer.

Everyone laughed, to which the officer said, without a smile, "I didn't say you could laugh." I guess he really was an officer.

The first thing the US Army does is classify you according to your skills and their needs. This involves psychological testing and medical evaluation. During the medical evaluation, my temperature was taken, so being a curious young guy, I looked at the reading. That was a mistake. I was immediately pulled out of that room and taken to another room where all the soldiers were bent over with thermometers stuck up their asses. "You want to play doctor, you can do that here," the medic said with a mocking smile.

Being in the military wasn't all about discipline, it was also about camaraderie. This was how I came to be double-timing and chanting an army ditty to boost our morale.

> "I gotta girl in Panama City, she's got whiskey in her titty, sound off, sound off, one, two, three, four, one two three four."

I learned rapidly that there are two kinds of soldiers in the US Army: those that receive orders, and those that give orders. Giving orders seemed a lot more practical because you didn't have to do all the dirty work, you could just order a lower-ranking soldier to do it. Your job was to make sure the work gets done. It's like when you see a group of men (always men) digging a hole—there will be only one or two men doing the digging, while the others are supervising and smoking cigarettes. I wasn't interested in the smoking, but the supervising sure looked good.

I also learned about the realities of life in the racially segregated Southern US. I had never been subject to racial discrimination or seen it with persons of a different race or color. Now it was staring me in my face. The training camp was in Baton Rouge, Louisiana, where the rules were vastly different than they had been in New York or Los Angeles.

I couldn't have been more shocked to see bathrooms labeled "colored," and water fountains labeled "colored," and on another corner, identical bathrooms and water fountains labeled "whites only." In my English naivety, I didn't understand at first why they needed separate bathrooms. But then again, I wasn't that familiar with American history when it came to things like that. I quickly got a crash course in segregation and learned which lines could be crossed, and which ones couldn't.

Alcohol was another story altogether. That was a line that got crossed frequently and repeatedly. Much of Louisiana was "dry," which meant if liquor touched your lips, then you were breaking the law. But we all knew that a quick word with one of the omnipresent taxi drivers could get you any hard liquor you desired.

Some soldiers didn't even bother with this solution and chose to buy "moonshine," a deadly concoction of pure alcohol distilled often through lead pipes. The Army set up a massive campaign to deter soldiers from drinking this stuff, with stories of soldiers going blind. But people did anyway. I didn't drink the 'shine, but I got my share of regular stuff. Alcohol had already become a regular part of my life. It wasn't bad yet, but it was going to be.

In their infinite wisdom, the US Army had decided that I would drive big trucks. It wasn't because I knew how to drive big trucks; I didn't even have a driver's license. (Apparently the Army assumed that every soldier was licensed to drive.). It was because there was a shortage of soldiers able to drive big trucks. That's how one day I was assigned to pick up a lowboy truck and trailer from the motor pool. It was a gigantic 40-foot tractor-trailer with more gears than two cars combined.

Slowly, I inched this monster truck out of the pitch-black bay and carefully got it to its destination nearby. Drawing upon my limited experience driving a 1958 Ford Escort in England, I somehow figured out the gears while double clutching and making grinding gear noises that alerted everyone in my path.

I could hear some soldiers laughing as I tried to back it up into a tight space. Managing that monster was hard work. At the end of the day, I was drenched in sweat. But I finally returned it undamaged and in one piece. Then I was handed a small piece of paper, which was my permit to drive just about anything the US Army had. It appeared that I had finished my training and testing in one day, all on my own.

Next, the US Army thought that I would be a great armored personnel carrier (APC) driver. This time, they actually did train me, because the carriers were more expensive than the trucks and they didn't want just any Tom, Dick, or Harry destroying their prized equipment.

A short time later, I got my own brand-new APC. But I couldn't cruise around the city streets and show off my new set of wheels. By this point I was stationed in Fort Benning, Georgia, and the only streets where I could perform my stunts were on the unpaved red clay, back roads of rural Fort Benning,

Georgia. One of my favorite tricks was to drive about 45 MPH and then make a sudden 90° turn. This was a lot of fun when I had a full load of unsuspecting US Army Officer Candidates in the back. I gave them several seconds warning about the turn, but few paid attention. After a few turns, though, they listened to every word I spoke.

Showing the US Army how to shoot

My big break in the Army came when I figured out that I already had a rare skill that few other soldiers could offer. During my time in England, I had become very proficient in shooting a pistol. I pointed out to the US Army Marksmanship Training Unit (USAMTU) that I was a skilled pistol shooter. They looked at each other and pointed out that half the US Army were skilled pistol shooters. "Ah," I said, "but I can shoot an international free pistol .22 caliber at 50 yards." Now, that got their attention.

So, they said they would transfer me for a week and see what I could do. All I had to do was shoot for a few hours per day and, at the week's end, bring in the paper targets that I had shot. I spent hours at the firing range every day, shooting so many targets that my fingers would feel like they were on fire. But I figured it was simple: they wanted paper targets showing good shooting, so I would give them what they wanted. I sorted out all the best targets and threw away all the bad ones. I placed them in a large envelope, sealed it, and gave it to the officer in charge.

I guess it was good enough, because a week later, I received orders that I had been assigned to the Marksmanship Training Unit for six months. I started preparing for the International Games in Wiesbaden, Germany. It was a great opportunity. But before I could get to compete in that, there were the tryouts in Camp Bullis, Texas, where the best from all the armed services and civilian shooters would compete for international placement.

USAMTU didn't have anyone in line to shoot international free pistol at that time, and they asked me if I would do it as it was a new category for them. What do you think I said to them, "I'll think about it?" Of course not. I was only a low-ranking soldier but had a chance to represent the US Army in an international competition. I immediately said, "Yes, sir!"

Camp Bullis, Texas, in the middle of summer was not an ideal environment. The heat and the bugs were incredible. With large flying insects swooping around my face, and sweat dripping everywhere, I wasn't at my best. This resulted in only average target scores, meaning I didn't get to go to Germany after all. But the USAMTU still kept me for the six months before sending me back to my original US Army unit. I ranked in the top 200 pistol shooters in the United States and got to spend half a year training with a special unit, so I didn't feel too bad.

Back at my base army unit (Company A, 58th Infantry, 197th Brigade), I volunteered for the Honor Guard. This meant that I got to dress up in my smartest uniform, with a rifle in hand, and fire several blank shots while standing at attention in funerals for deceased soldiers. Most of these young soldiers had died in Vietnam and left young children and wives in their quest to serve their country. Some of the young wives fainted or just collapsed on the ground. This was a reality we had to deal with as professional soldiers. But however unpleasant it was to stand at a funeral with a grieving family, it was better than being the guest of honor.

After the funeral, we would stop on the way back to Fort Benning, in our olive-drab-painted school bus—a clearly marked military vehicle. Once, we stopped at a small cafe, in uniform, with M14 rifles in tow. We were told that we were welcome, but the black soldiers in our group, the cafe owners called them colored, would not be admitted.

Our sergeant got on the radio to the base, and everyone heard the response. If necessary, the US Army would come down and surround the cafe until such time as we were all admitted. I never did find out if that was just a bluff because we all entered the cafe, and everyone was all smiles as if nothing had happened. Maybe racial segregation was still a line people didn't cross down south, but apparently, the US Army could cross any line it pleased.

My platoon sergeant liked to leave early on Fridays to play golf. One day he asked me if I would do the squad formation for him on Friday afternoons. This meant that at noon we would all assemble and be accounted for each day. I gladly agreed. No problem,

I thought. After a month of doing him this favor, I decided it was time my back was scratched too. I asked him what it would take to become a "buck" sergeant Non-Commissioned Officer E5 rank. He told me he would put my name forward, and the board would assess me personally.

Weeks later, three stripes were pinned on my fatigues, much to the amazement of my fellow soldiers. I was now a fully-fledged leader and Non-Commissioned Officer and could tell them what to do—which I did frequently.

I'm in charge now

The longer I stayed in the US Army, the more I figured out how to work the system. One of my favorite techniques was to carry a clipboard under my arm. Whenever I felt it necessary, I could start writing on the clipboard and no one dared to interfere with my work whatever that was or was not.

On weekends, several of my soldier friends and I would get together and drive to Panama City, Florida. The driver was, we found out later, the son of a Mafioso man, and he had this great set of sparkling wheels: a 55 Chevy. It was beautiful, green, big and strong, with massive chrome bumpers that could hoover up women like a strong magnet.

We needed something to get women's attention, because it was obvious that we were soldiers (we couldn't conceal the haircuts no matter what we wore).

And the fact that we were soldiers meant that we were only after one thing in the eyes of the girls. Our reputation preceded us everywhere we went.

One evening we were driving around the dimly lit streets of Panama City's bar area when something caught our eye, and the driver decided to make a U-turn in the wide street. He didn't see the police car parked in front of a bar and backed right into it. Only then did he realize that he'd hit something with a large sheriff's star painted on the side.

We quickly drove away and minutes later came back to see a sheriff scratching his head, looking at a huge dent on the side panel, and letting out a lot of words that I never learned in school. We pulled over to check the Chevy, but there wasn't any sign of damage; the chrome bumpers were tougher than Panama City. We drove back to the base confident that we had increased the income of a local auto body repair shop and thereby improved the economy as a result of the driver's carelessness. All in all, a good weekend.

The girls we met on the weekends were almost always in groups. This allowed us to tell them that we were not just after one thing, but several things. This generally broke the ice, and we got lucky often enough, but things were difficult if we all wanted the same girl. There were occasions when we flipped a coin to see who would be the lucky one. That didn't always work either, because the girls invariably saw right through these games, and when that happened, none of us got lucky.

Saying goodbye to the US Army

In my last few days in the US Army, I started pushing boundaries again, figuring I could get away with some cheeky stuff. When an officer was in sight, not only did I salute him, but I also said, "Short, Sir," which usually provoked, under his breath, "lucky bastard!" or something similar, because the officer knew that I was leaving soon and he would have a lot more time to go before he could get out.

While I did enjoy my time in the US Army, when my Expiration Time of Service arrived, like a caged animal in a zoo, I definitely felt ready to be released into the general population of civilians. But it didn't take me long to realize how much I had changed in terms of discipline and personality. Time in the army institutionalizes an individual, and that person needs to be reconditioned to return to civilian life. I was no different.

The US Army did try to get me to re-enlist, or "re-up," as they called it. A group of us were taken up in a helicopter, given the grand tour, and offered the opportunity to train as helicopter pilots, thereby becoming officers. But none of us took them up on the offer because we had all heard there was a shortage of helicopter pilots mostly because they were being shot down in Vietnam.

I asked them if I could train as a fixed-wing pilot instead, but they said no, so I declined to re-up. I learned much later that I made the right decision. Signing up again would have meant remaining in the US Army for an additional three years.

All good things end, and my two years of compulsory draft service finally came to an end. I was quite surprised when a vehicle arrived to take me to the airport. I'm not sure whether they were glad to finally see the back of me, or they genuinely wanted to help me. Maybe both.

My parents were especially pleased to see me when I returned to London because I had narrowly escaped being sent to Vietnam while in the US Army. It turned out that because I was not a citizen of the US yet, a complete background check was done on me to make sure that I wasn't a British spy or something equally sinister.

After about fourteen months, the "dossier" on me was finally completed. I saw it and signed it but was refused a copy of my life history because it was secret. It was secret from prying eyes, but available to me on a read-only basis.

As a result, there was insufficient time to send me to Vietnam within my two years of service. So, my parents were understandably apprehensive when I told them I would be going to Vietnam at the height of the war as a civilian contractor. But I was an adult and felt that I could make decisions for myself regardless of the potential consequences. I was first shipped off to Stuttgart, Germany, where I got vaccinated for every possible disease known to man. I know that it was for every possible disease because I felt like I had the flu for almost a week.

In Stuttgart, Germany, I learned everything I needed to know before I left for Vietnam two months later. What they taught me was not something I didn't already know. What they failed to tell me was that it was as dangerous as hell, and I could get killed. No one ever takes on a mission where they know they have a 100 percent chance of being killed unless this philosophy is ingrained in their culture.

But the lure of danger and excitement is inherent in many of us; dying is not something we take seriously, that happens to other less fortunate people. This is why the military around the world can recruit young men, and sometimes women, to engage in dangerous locations and hot spots. The flashy television commercials are nothing like the horror of war; but the young people find out about that later.

The time came when I was due to fly out to Vietnam via Pan Am, which coincidentally involved a stopover in London. When my parents said goodbye to me, it felt like they would never see me again, and the tears flowed without shame on all sides.

PART 3

Vietnam

What do you do after two years of military service? Travel, of course. During a stop back home in London, I was intrigued by an ad that called for civilians to serve overseas as a military contractor. Little did I know I'd be risking my life, stationed near the front lines in Vietnam.

Asia beckons: plentiful and delicious food and girls

It was ironic that I'd managed to spend all my time as an enlisted man safely in the US, and only got sent to the war zone after becoming a civilian again. There were definitely benefits to working as a representative civilian contractor for Chrysler Military Sales Corporation: armed with a Non-Combatant ID card, which showed I had an equivalent rank of Lieutenant Colonel or GS 13E, having made huge leaps in rank and pay. I didn't have to do the grunt work that the soldiers did. Less work, more pay, and an exotic location: seemed like a good deal to me. If it weren't for the fact that there was a war going on, it would have been a great adventure; however, misadventure was closer to the mark.

Vietnam in the thick of the war was hot, sticky, dirty and dangerous, and that was just the streets! Soldiers strolled around the streets of Saigon unarmed, which I thought strange for a war zone. Beggars approached out of nowhere, and vehicles were driven around at breakneck speed. Your life was only worth $50 if you had the misfortune to cross the wrong person.

But not everything was bad. The ratio of women to men was five to one, which meant that you didn't have to chase after girls, they chased after you. It became more of a selection process in your favor. This was a far cry from cruising the streets of Panama City trying to win over girls who didn't always care for soldiers. And the food was much better. Just because a war was going on didn't mean that food was scarce, far from it, the food—like the girls—was plentiful and delicious. Actually, anything was available if you were willing to pay the price.

Nighttime bars saw scores of women trying to entice young guys to part with their money. The guys were up for anything, and so were most of the women. But there was a 10 p.m. curfew, so most bars were thinning out earlier to give everyone a chance to return to their base or hotel.

Vietnam is where drinking went from an occasional hobby to a daily ritual for me. Life was dangerous there, and people did what they always do in the face of danger: try and have a good time while they can. There was plenty of whiskey for thirsty soldiers looking for a good time. And what's more, the girls could easily outdrink you. Besides that, there were usually two girls with each guy. When they each placed their delicate fingers on the guys' legs, and their minds became scrambled with the alcohol, they probably knew at that point that they had lost control of the situation, and were putty in the hands of the girls, but the guys were past caring. This was when a lot of soldiers lost all the money they were carrying. That never happened to me though, but I confess I still drank more than my share of whiskey. The money in my pocket, however, remained intact.

The bars were wild: there was an atmosphere that almost anything goes. In one bar I visited, a westerner attracted a lot of attention by putting live cockroaches in his mouth while out of sight, then sitting at the bar, and allowing the cockroaches to slip out of his mouth to the utter shock and amazement of the staff and patrons.

Everyone played hard because they knew that day could be their last.

In all my time in Vietnam, I never paid for a girl. They would naturally flock to me like bees to honey. My biggest problem was scheduling the ones I wanted so that none of them appeared at the same time and the same place. Fortunately, I was well versed in logistics and planning and managed to sort it out without risking my neck or other bodily parts getting severely damaged. Finally, I thought, I could put my hard-earned organizational skills to good use.

But it wasn't all fun and games. If I make it sound like Vietnam was all play, it wasn't—the worst was yet to come.

After a short stint in Saigon, I was transferred to Dong Tam Base in the Mekong Delta. I had thought Saigon was a lot to take in, but the Delta was sensory overload. Loud, hot, and cramped, it wasn't exactly luxurious. I was housed in an old wooden barracks with little accommodation for privacy. Not what I was expecting. I was told that there was insufficient billeting for US Army Officers, let alone civilians, so it was take it or leave it. I took it.

Dong Tam Base Bunker, Vietnam, 1969.

Someone has to do the dirty work, but it won't be me

My work was administrative, meaning I didn't do any hard, manual work to damage my newly manicured nails that cost me $1. (Other extra personal services I didn't need were performed behind a discreet curtain.) My work involved obtaining vehicles for soldiers leaving Vietnam, lots of messy paperwork with carbon paper, before mailing this information to HQ. In between these were trips to the mess hall where everyone met up. It kept me busy, but I was hardly suffering.

On one of these trips, I noticed a "Huey" helicopter—a Bell UH-1—approaching slowly. Slung from the landing rails was a net. As the Huey got closer, I could see blood dripping from the bodies inside the net. There were likely 20 or more bodies being delivered to the Graves Registration Unit nearby. Each day, scenes like this occurred in the battle zone of the Mekong Delta. That wasn't something you saw in the streets of Saigon. Is it any wonder we all drank so much?

Many nights, Dong Tam—the local base and home to the 9th Infantry Division, US Army—would receive a barrage of mortar shells from outside the perimeter. If you were a general or high-ranking officer, you had the luxury and comparative safety of a fortified bunker. Alas, I had no such thing, and when the ear-piercing siren gave its warning blast of incoming rounds, I put on my strategically placed sandals and hauled ass to the nearby bunker in just my shorts. Not a relaxing way to live.

I was minding my own business and reading a book, I don't even remember what kind of book it was, one late evening on Dong Tam Base, Vietnam, in March 1969, when there was an almighty explosion. This was no ordinary incoming round; this was like the whole ground opened up and shook everyone and everything in its wake. All the sirens went off on the base as if to signify that the jackpot had been won. It had been won, but not by the troops on the base.

It had always been the stuff of nightmares that the massive ammunition dump could be hit, but that had never happened until now. Was it just luck or skill? Rumors were flying that the Viet Cong planned this and got lucky with one strike.

It was common knowledge that Viet Cong prisoners were taken up in helicopters, where the pilots would then steeply bank the chopper to one side. The seatbelt of the Viet Cong prisoner next to the door would not have been fastened, and then the remaining prisoners had the misfortune to listen to their comrade's blood-curdling screams as he plummeted through the sky towards certain mincemeat. The horror felt by the Viet Cong prisoners was even more magnified by the look of absolute terror on the face of the departing prisoner.

When they returned to base, minus one and were questioned by Vietnamese interrogators, they instantly had diarrhea of the mouth. Any hesitation and they were threatened with another one-way ride in the chopper. No one ever went for a second ride. Unsurprisingly, no one ever directly admitted doing this either, but after conversations with low-ranking and high-ranking soldiers, it definitely happened. But the stories were always about someone else doing that, not themselves.

There, will, undoubtedly, be people who question the ethics of such practices, and while I personally don't condone them, I can understand what motivated these soldiers to take extreme measures. War changes how people perceive ethics. You have to walk in that person's shoes before you can judge them. In a hypothetical scenario, a soldier's mother is told that her son's life is in mortal danger. The hypothetical scenario is that a Viet Cong soldier can eliminate that danger but won't talk. Do you seriously believe that the mother will insist that the VC's human rights are not violated? Of course not, the mother will tell them to do whatever you need to do to bring back my son safely. Torture is always carried out by other people; it's called "plausible deniability."

People expect, in those situations, that the military or government will do the dirty work, but just don't tell me the details. And that's how much of the war in Vietnam was fought—dirty. Historians record what happened from the data and reports available to them, (usually not firsthand) but the people who were there, on the ground, know the facts and real history, which is often different and conflicts with the official version.

History is recorded in three ways, what actually occurred, a country's official version of what occurred, and the rest of the world's version of what occurred. Very seldom do these versions align with each other. You choose which version of history suits you best.

Murder and suicide: All in a night's work

One night the war really visited my doorstep. I had settled in for the night in my barracks, when I was awakened by a tremendous bang, followed by dense smoke and screaming I shall never forget. The upstairs of the barracks had taken a hit, and I was met with the horrific aftermath. Decapitated bodies were strewn around, while others had limbs torn from their bodies; everyone else on the floor had cuts and broken bones—less life-threatening, but their blood-curdling screams were just as bad.

I thought we'd been hit by a shell. All was not what it seemed, however. Instead of an incoming enemy mortar round, it was a drug-crazed soldier, high on marijuana, who had decided to play around with a live grenade.

Drugs were in rampant use by many soldiers. Nobody cared until it was time for a soldier's assignment or tour of duty to end. Then they cared. No soldier could leave Vietnam with drug usage showing in their system—it made the Army look bad. But until then, all bets were off. As with the tobacco from my youth, I avoided the hard stuff, and congratulated myself on doing so. I was drinking, of course, more than ever, but in my mind that didn't really count.

To avoid bad publicity in Vietnam and the growing angry public in the United States, the whole matter of suicide and murder was written off as enemy activity. Every soldier involved, whether dead or alive, was decorated with a slew of medals, and the ones who survived were ordered to keep their mouths shut, under penalty of court-martial, to maintain morale.

This wasn't an unusual situation for the Army. Fragging, or throwing a grenade at an officer or NCO was not uncommon. When officers or NCOs seemingly endangered those under their command, those under their command believed their only way to stay alive was to remove the threat. More than a hundred officers and NCOs were murdered this way, resulting in officers and NCOs becoming more careful in their decision-making on the battlefield. A few soldiers even told me that they had considered fragging but changed their minds as the situation on the battlefield improved.

I didn't want to stay in the same building with these drug-addled soldiers anymore, but there was nothing the US Army could do for me other than suggest I remove myself from the base and find accommodations in the nearby town of Mỹ Tho. I found a civilian contractor, Eric, and his Vietnamese wife, who agreed to put me up in their house on the edge of town. The house was basic, to say the least, with, strangely, a tent set up in one room, but it seemed a safe alternative to the barracks on the base. They had a cute young maid who took care of the cleaning, cooking, laundry, shopping and many other things I was yet to discover.

After I had settled in, I asked where I would be sleeping. The maid in her broken English said, "You sleep tent." Since it was the only place that had any sort of bed, I inquired where would she sleep. She said, "I sleep tent." Wait a minute, I thought, doesn't this mean we both sleep in the tent? Perhaps there had been a misunderstanding. But indeed, that night when I went into the tent, she came in also. There had been no mis-communication: my new accommodations apparently came with a girl. Following my military training, I thought it best to do as I was told, be a good boy, and get with the program.

The arrangement in this house was fine with me, but there was just one slight problem with my new quarters: I needed to drive from the house in Mỹ Tho, during daylight hours only, to the sprawling Dong Tam Base through areas heavily occupied by the Viet Cong, using a VW bug. As a civilian, I was advised to ignore the Viet Cong if I saw them; and I saw them often with AK-47s slung over their shoulders and bandoliers of ammunition weighing them down. Being an unarmed contractor driving an unarmored VW bug, I thought ignoring the heavily armed enemy was a good idea.

Living in that house wasn't really that bad for me at first. It was almost like having a full-service apartment, except I was living in a tent in the middle of a house, in a war-torn country, with a girl I barely knew. The house also had a crazed man and a soon-to-be-dead wife, but I didn't know that.

The maid and I got along fine. I increased her salary, which was about $50 per month. She only worked for a few hours in the evening, so I thought it fair to pay an extra amount plus some pocket money for her expenses; she seemed quite happy with this. Each day she washed and set my clothes out for me, which was good because I often had to change several times per day thanks to the extreme temperatures and humidity.

The maid did a great job with the laundry, but the local water supply wasn't all that clean. I soon came down with, quarter-sized, itchy ringworm marks on one leg. I stood in the back of a line of soldiers waiting in the Dong Tam base doctor's office. The soldiers looked a motley lot, stooped over while grabbing their crotches as if they were in a Michael Jackson video.

The doctor called me to the front and gave me priority over the soldiers, who no doubt, were mostly waiting for their painful shots of penicillin to treat their gonorrhea. A lot of it must have been going around, because a large sign in the office proclaimed: DO YOU DRIP, DO YOU BURN, TAKE A SEAT, AND WAIT YOUR TURN. But that wasn't me. I was just given a cream and sent on my way.

Sometimes on the base I would visit the officers club and have a drink at the bar. One day the barman on duty, an enlisted man, asked how I had managed to survive the drive from Mỹ Tho to Dong Tam Base.

"What do you mean?" I asked.

"Do you know that soldiers have been shot at while driving?" he responded. This was, in fact, news to me. I was used to seeing armed Viet Cong, but nobody had shot at me yet. "Don't you have a weapon?" he continued.

"No," I admitted.

"Do you want one? For $50, I can have a .45 for you in a couple of days," he said while nonchalantly mixing a drink. "They're always picking up dead helicopter pilots, so it shouldn't be a problem."

I tried not to think about plundering pistols off dead airmen and wondered whether he had just said that for effect; but that was the reality of war. People died, and you just moved on.

He convinced me that it would be a good idea to arm myself, and now my briefcase was brimming to capacity. It was already stuffed with my small typewriter, numerous forms with carbon paper, a small adding machine and a Minolta 16mm camera. Added to this now were a heavy .45 caliber pistol and a fair amount of rounds to go with it—spoils of war.

Looking down the barrel of a .45

It wasn't long after this when I noticed things started to go missing at the house where I was staying. A bottle of Chivas Regal Scotch here, a little money there. I didn't pay much attention at first, because I was extremely busy. But when the pistol went missing, I had had enough. I complained to the homeowner, Eric, and he said he would talk with his wife that evening. Eric lived with his common-law Vietnamese wife, one girl about eight and one boy about nine. These children were from the wife's previous marriage. Between them, they also had a baby boy, six months old.

When I came home that evening, I heard some loud arguing at the back of the house, followed by the distinctive sound of a .45 caliber pistol shot. I rushed in and saw Eric's wife crumpled on the floor with blood oozing onto the white tiled floor from a huge gaping hole that had once been her head. Instead of a living human being, she was now a body, lots of blood, and bits of bone resembling chicken wishbones with lumps of grey matter. All of his children were present when Eric shot his wife, fatally, in the head allegedly by accident.

I stared at Eric, who was still holding the pistol.

"Why?" was all I could think to say.

"She lied to me," he said. "She covered for the maid."

There was an eerie silence, and then he pointed the pistol at me and demanded that I drive him to Saigon immediately. This, of course, was impossible, since there was a curfew at 10 p.m., and we were fast approaching that hour. Luckily, I was able to reason with him and explain that no matter what course of action he took, it would be worse if he left the scene with me in tow. In addition, I thought to myself, I didn't want to be charged as an accomplice.

After what seemed like an eternity, a joint Vietnamese/American military patrol showed up. They interviewed Eric, listened to his story of a gun "accidentally" firing, and promptly confiscated the pistol. Of course, you must realize that the trigger pull weight of a 1911A1 pistol is usually between 5 and 6½ pounds, which makes accidental firing unlikely. Being remarkably familiar with firearms, especially the .45, I knew that it was much more likely that the pistol was fired deliberately, because the trigger weight is so heavy. But I wasn't in the room when the shot was fired, and I didn't see what happened.

When I entered the room after the shooting, the two children remained remarkably and extremely calm, under the circumstances; they just lit some incense sticks and started praying. Not a tear ran from their cheeks. I can only imagine how in later life they must have struggled with the knowledge that their father shot their mother to death; whether they believed it was an accident, only they know. The next day they were taken away by the mother's family except for the baby who remained with Eric. I have my own opinion of how it happened, but I've kept that to myself.

Surprisingly, neither the maid nor I were questioned. No photographs or measurements were taken, and the body was removed. Within minutes and out of nowhere, a woman appeared with a mop and bucket and cleaned up the grisly remains. I was led into my own car and escorted to a hotel in town as if nothing had ever happened. Eric was taken away for questioning and eventual trial.

The next afternoon, I returned to the house to gather my belongings, but there was almost nothing left to collect. Most of my clothes and personal possessions had been swiftly removed by the wife's family. I didn't care. I just wanted to put this horrible event behind me, and that's exactly what I did.

The thieving maid who started all the trouble walked away as if her hands were clean. When I relocated to Saigon, I took with me three remaining bottles of Chivas Regal Scotch. But each time I drank from those bottles, it reminded me of the whole awful affair. I never bought Chivas Regal again.

Six months later in downtown Saigon, I ran into Eric on the street. He told me that his lawyer knew the judge very well and that the judge had a huge admiration for everything American—in particular, portraits of Benjamin Franklin. In fact, the more Franklins the judge saw, the happier he was. In short, Eric left the courthouse a free man. He pointed out his new girlfriend who was window shopping on the other side of the street, and I wondered if she knew what kind of man he really was. Should I tell her? I was conflicted. Then I decided that I had no business interfering in their lives. What would I tell her? "Did you know your boyfriend shot his wife in the head, in front of his children, and bribed his way out of jail?" Would she even believe me? Would I end up with another gun pointed at my face? I couldn't change history; I could only learn from it.

How to live in a war zone without getting your head blown off

When I told my Gia Long Street office in Saigon of my experiences at Eric's house, they just laughed it off and told me that I had been a busy man. I realized at that moment that they didn't really care whether someone lived or died.

If you lived, it would all be laughed off, leaving you with memories to recount later. If you died, then you would be shipped home in an aluminum casket with a name tag on your big toe.

"No worries, John, we have something better for you," they said encouragingly.

And they weren't wrong. My new place was luxurious compared to all the previous housing. It was the top floor of a four-story building in an elegant tree-lined street designed by former French Colonialists. The building, named "Hergert BOQ," was "bachelor officers quarters" reserved for officers with the rank of Lieutenant Colonel, civilian and military. It was definitely comfortable, and even had a mess hall where you could get American-style meals at rock bottom prices when you got tired of eating Asian food (I rarely did, but it was nice to have the option of something different). It was a home away from home for American officers and civilian contractors.

The front of the building boasted the ubiquitous Vietnamese armed military guard, which supposedly added to our safety, although many times the guards were caught with their eyes closed as they guarded their posts; but we never knew how often this happened because none of us stayed awake to watch them.

At the front desk was the ever-present Madame Hoa, a woman in her forties, hair in a bun that never came down, who saw all the comings and goings and was pleased to accommodate your requests so long as her palm was greased with silver. If it wasn't, your life could get extremely complicated if you were a social kind of person, which I was.

I had a suspicion that she might have been a North Vietnamese intelligence agent because of her appearance and accent, but I never mentioned this dangerous thought to anyone while I was there. Perhaps, I thought, her presence was the reason the Viet Cong never attacked the building.

Another popular officers' haunt was the Rex Hotel in downtown Saigon. High-ranking male officers and civilians could bring their female friends there and drink and dance with absolute discretion and security. It was well known that most of the officers were married, but nobody cared. This was a war zone and all the normal rules of social engagement were broken. Signs were posted: "No Photographs." This was strictly enforced. If you were married or unmarried and wanted a Polaroid of Ms. Suzy Creamcheese and yourself, it would have to be taken elsewhere.

Now I was settled in a reasonably safe place in Saigon, it was time to find out more about what the city had to offer. For years Saigon had been known as the "Pearl of the Orient;" the city had a certain mystique that I was eager to explore. One of the things I was able to start enjoying was the exclusive Cercle Sportif Club. Although they claimed that they were accepting you rather than you were accepting them, as soon as I mentioned the Hergert BOQ, doors magically opened.

I had full access to fencing, tennis, martial arts, and a large swimming pool. I particularly enjoyed the martial arts, and quickly excelled in judo and aikido, achieving a green belt in judo and an orange belt in aikido. Most of my judo opponents were European and brown belt qualified. It wasn't long before I learned to become extra defensive with these pros; I had to, because they often sent me flying, and landing badly, seeing nothing but stars.

Hergert Bachelor Officers Quarters room 24, Saigon, Vietnam, 1970. (Polaroid). I was quite thirsty in those days!

The swimming pool was a great place to hang out and relax. While I was never much into swimming, being more like a cat who didn't swim until it was pushed into the water, I didn't mind soaking up the atmosphere, especially because I could watch a bevy of beauties strutting their stuff around the pool in swimsuits.

It wasn't long before I caught the eye of one of them. It turns out that she was a Bác Sĩ, or doctor. But not just any doctor: she was also a surgeon who was fluent in French and English.

Vietnamese girls didn't waste any time with niceties such as dinner, dancing, or the movies. They got right down to the nitty-gritty: try before you buy. I was quite surprised when this young doctor invited herself to my place that same evening. I realized that I still needed to adjust myself to the difference in cultures.

Dr. P. became a regular visitor to my place. Whenever she visited, she had to leave early each evening because overnight visitors were not allowed in my building and the city had a 10 p.m. curfew. But she came back, nonetheless. I thought things were going well. I even met her well-to-do family, who lived in a luxury villa provided by the government; her father was a senior Vietnamese civil servant. However, she told me later that her mother said that, because I was a Westerner, she considered her own daughter to be a prostitute. I never returned to see the mother.

One day Dr. P. came to see me, and her face looked as if it had been drained of all color. She told me that the young family maid had borrowed some of Dr. P.'s birth control pills without her knowledge or consent, and later replaced them, unknowingly, with counterfeit pills she had bought from an unscrupulous pharmacy. Dr. P. unwittingly took the fake pills and became pregnant. She now needed $400 to get an abortion. She didn't get the maid fired, because it would also make her look bad with her parents. She did, however, make the maid work extra until such time as she believed the maid had learned her lesson. I was beginning to realize that hiring a maid was a risky business.

Dr. P. told me that occasionally, the Viet Cong would come to her house at night, demanding money. I asked her whether there was anything she could do about it, and she told me to keep it quiet since they were her cousins. Dr. P. knew that to report them would be tantamount to a death sentence, even though they were family.

Be careful how you choose your friends

This wasn't unusual. Many Vietnamese families had relatives who were secretly members of the Viet Cong, who were everywhere. I had some French friends who had rubber plantations and restaurants in the region near Saigon; they told me that they would love to invite me to the plantations, but since the Viet Cong were frequent uninvited social visitors who would stop by for a coffee and chat, for my safety, it might not be a good idea. I agreed with them and stayed away.

Years later, I discovered that the French plantation owners were actually forced to store millions of US dollars in large boxes containing $100 bills that helped fuel the war effort. The Viet Cong were able to get away with this because Americans and foreigners' properties were rarely searched. Even when the properties were "clean," it was standard practice to pay everybody off just to leave you alone. This money came from huge black-market operations that involved currency manipulation of the "script" used by the military to counter speculation. It didn't work, of course; rather than discourage speculation, the script only increased it.

Also, the Viet Cong would buy large quantities of fuel from the Vietnamese military (ARVN), and use it on their tanks and other vehicles. Even if they didn't use all the fuel, they could resell it despite the distinctive dye it was colored with and make a large profit. Profit, greed, and corruption were so widespread that it was impossible to prevent or stop it.

Ultimately, this contributed to the inability and unwillingness of the ARVN to fight their own battles. The corruption was rampant, and it was easier to lean on the support of the US Army to fight on their behalf. This made a victory inevitable for the North Vietnamese. They paid dearly for that victory: they lost over a million soldiers, compared to 58,000 American casualties (not counting the hundreds of thousands of Vietnamese ARVN soldiers and more civilians). But in the end, despite their heavier losses, the Viet Cong were willing to pay the price for victory, and the US was not.

"I promise you won't feel a thing; I'm just going to cut your leg off."

Dr. P. was only 24 years old and already a surgeon. I asked her how this could be possible. She told me that there were so many war casualties that she learned surgery through on-the-job training, unlike the way it is in Western countries that are consumed by regulation and lawsuits.

Her job seemed like a nightmare to me. This was wartime surgery, not elective procedures done in a fancy hospital. If a casualty came in with a leg completely shattered, she would be expected to amputate it and quickly move on to the next patient. She told me that she was quite able to separate her work from her personal life, but I don't know how she was able to sleep at night.

There was no such thing as calling for a "qualified surgeon." If you were the doctor on call, you were the only available doctor to save the patient. Minutes often separated the patient from life or death. If the patient died, and it was because of your inexperience, next time, you would just try not to repeat your mistakes.

Families of the patient readily accepted this without looking for lawyers. You were the doctor, and as such, your experience and judgment were not called into question. All hospitals routinely accepted patients in any condition and were expected to perform miracles when often there was no hope of survival.

The gruesome nature of her work notwithstanding, I enjoyed my time with Dr. P. She was young and pretty and made me feel rather good. Everything was fun until she asked me one day, quite suddenly, a question that changed everything:

"Do you love me?"

I didn't know what to say. Like most people in Saigon, I was used to living for the moment. Love didn't enter into it.

"No," I stammered.

From that moment on, it was a rapid journey downhill.

Whatever love is

My relationship with Dr. P. came to a crashing halt, but as an American living in a luxurious and secure location in Saigon, I wasn't lonely for long. Out of nowhere, another girl appeared on the scene. We were together for a while, until she told me that her family was moving to another part of Vietnam. Not too long after, I received a letter from her telling me how much she missed me, and that she was now pregnant by me. At the end of this beautifully scripted letter, which I should have kept, she asked me whether she should KILL or KEEP the baby. By now my brain was exploding with all the things happening to me. I'd been through a lot of ups and downs in a short amount of time.

So, I did the only thing possible under the circumstances: I dug my head into the sand. I talked this over with some male friends, and they all offered the same advice. If she really is pregnant with my baby and goes ahead with the birth, she will let me know. If she's bluffing and not pregnant, I won't hear any more. If she is pregnant and has a termination, I won't hear any more. So, the "won't hear any mores" outweighed the one "hear more." Of course, my friends were right, and I never heard any more from her.

With all the stressful things I was going through, I also stepped up my drinking. This wasn't a good thing to do, but at the time, it seemed like the right thing to do.

Everyone knows that to qualify for US citizenship, you must be a resident in the US for five years. What I didn't realize was that my status and residency in Vietnam, during the Vietnam war, counted toward my five years required in the US. So, in 1970, I hopped on a military flight to Agana, Guam, and became a citizen after five years exactly; goodbye "green card," hello green passport.

PART 4

America

My time in Vietnam finally came to an end. I'd had some good times, mixed with a lot of bad ones. In hindsight, I'm lucky I didn't get my head blown off over there. But I didn't. I came out of it alive and whole, mostly. The scars I'd picked up in Vietnam, you couldn't see. I'd also picked up an addiction to alcohol that, while seemingly under control, was more than I was used to.

I was still restless, and not ready to head back to the UK. I'd eventually return to London, filled with mixed feelings about the danger and excitement of Vietnam. But after my turbulent time in Southeast Asia, the US was looking surprisingly good to me. Plus, I figured that America owed me a bit of peace and tranquility, after all I'd been through—first as a soldier, far from the war, and then as a contractor, smack in the middle of it.

I ended up back in Florida, where I'd spent a lot of fun weekends on leave as a soldier. I was thinking of how the Army hadn't wanted to let me train as an aircraft pilot. Well, I wasn't in the Army anymore. It was time to follow my interest in flying and consider a career as a pilot, as I'd always wanted. With that in mind, I took flying lessons at Burnside Ott Aviation in Miami. Learning to fly was a challenge, but I was used to challenges. And after navigating down the street in an armored personnel carrier, staying in the air was relatively easy; after all, there isn't anything to run into in the sky, unless you wander off course.

In less time than you'd believe, six weeks, I was a qualified private pilot. I had my license, but I didn't have my new career, unfortunately. The Federal Aviation Administration-certified doctor who issued my medical certificate said that the peripheral vision in my eyes was slightly under the standard requirement necessary for commercial pilots. I was, though, still qualified for private flying.

This was a great disappointment for me, but at least I'd given it a shot. The problem was, now I needed another plan. I figured that I could enrol in university.

John P. Culnane piloting a Cessna 150 at Miami, 1970s.

It would be a place where I could learn whatever skills I needed and decide on what career to follow next.

I found a place to live in Miami Springs, near one of the airports; the rent was cheap because renters put up with the constant noise of planes taking off and landing. Through a friend of a friend, I found an airline pilot who needed a roommate because he spent most of his time away in Central and South America.

I soon got to meet my neighbors, a husband and his wife who both worked in the airline industry. One day, after a coffee and some chit-chat, he asked me, now that I was new to the area, whether I needed anything.

Miami, 1970s. I couldn't afford a haircut.

He took me into his bedroom to show me his wares, where on the bed, were two large suitcases. He opened one and my eyes popped out of my head. Inside were hundreds of snub-nosed shiny revolvers, the ones known as "Saturday Night Specials."

"Would you like one?" he asked.

"Not sure about that," I said, not wanting to offend him. After all, he was a man with a giant pile of pistols in his bedroom.

"$50 each or two for $75," he said, like he was doing me a favor.

My mind raced back to Vietnam, with all the guns and killing that I had seen.

"I'll let you know," I said, absolutely certain that I would not be buying an illegal Saturday Night Special, let alone using one.

Miami, 1970s.

I was kind of curious about what was in the other suitcase. But I didn't have to wonder long because he opened it right afterwards. It was filled with precisely weighed bags of marijuana. By then, I had seen enough and excused myself, much to his disappointment. On my way out, he told me that every two weeks he returned to his hometown in a major Northeastern US city, to replenish his stock, courtesy of his airline employer that enabled him to travel for free. I made a mental reminder not to visit this neighbor ever again. I didn't care how often he replenished his stock; I was never going to be a customer.

Miami had the reputation of being an anything-goes party town. It was a far cry from war-torn Saigon, but there were still all kinds of unsavory activities. It was not unusual to hear about armed robberies and car-jackings and so forth. And it was common knowledge that cops would carry an untraceable gun as a backup or throw away in case they shot you accidentally, which to me sounds like an oxymoron because cops never shoot their guns accidentally: it's always on purpose. With a disposable, untraceable weapon, cops could throw away the extra gun and claim that you'd been armed. This was their get-out-of-jail card or insurance against false arrest; even when they were with a partner; the "Blue Code of Silence" meant they had a (lying, legal) witness to back them up.

Everyone in South Florida seemed to be carrying a gun. It was relatively easy for any individual to get a permit to carry a concealed weapon. Road rage was common in Miami, and some drivers resorted to flashing their guns at drivers who got in their way. This was how some irate drivers ended up getting shot by overzealous cops or other motorists who disliked guns shoved in their faces while they were going about their everyday business of driving.

University: Study time or party time?

Florida International University was a new institution with a wide range of programs. I decided to attend open enrolment day, where you could meet staff, select courses, and enrol on the spot. I went there with a rough idea of what I wanted to pursue but was immediately distracted by large numbers of young women hovering around particular courses. As a result, somehow, I found myself signed up for a sculpture class of mostly girls. It

1970s in Miami. It was the smallest car I could find!

was a fun way to start, but not an organized way to plan a college major.

I spent a couple of years taking classes filled with pretty women during the week and drinking on the weekends. It seemed like a great way to spend time, but it wasn't really getting me anywhere.

Once, I was sitting in one of my psychology classes at Florida International University, Miami, when I noticed the girl seated in front of me. She had long ash-blonde curly hair and blue eyes just like mine. She wore a tight green tee-shirt without a bra, and somehow, she had managed to pour herself into the tightest blue jeans imaginable.

She must have caught me staring at her and gave me a smile that seemed to say, "Do you like what you see?" I was almost glued to my seat and blurted out my name, "John," "Ms. E.," she said. At that point, I was completely oblivious as to what was going on in the classroom. There could have been a fire alarm and I wouldn't have noticed.

"Do you want to go over to the Ratskeller for a drink?" "Sure," she said in a husky voice. Later, after a few beers, she got close to me and said, "Wanna go over to my place?" And that's how it all started, smiles at the beginning of the relationship, and tears at the end.

Do what you have to do and don't look back

My father, then in his mid-sixties, had been suffering mini strokes; I thought it best to visit him before it was too late. Florida State University (FSU) had a summer program in London that matched up with my degree and schedule. But this would mean leaving Ms. E., to whom I was getting extremely attached. So much so that I believed that I was in love.

I had a dilemma: do I leave my girlfriend for six months, or do I visit my father whom I might never see again? I discussed this with Ms. E., but she dismissed my concerns, saying, "Do what you have to do." I deliberated for a long time before enrolling in the FSU London summer program. The trouble was I didn't tell Ms. E. until I was ready to leave. I just couldn't face her and maybe change my mind.

She reacted with shock and anger at my sudden departure. Although I'd discussed it with her early on, she felt I wasn't open with her and didn't like that I'd made the decision to go in secret. She said, "Don't expect me to be waiting for you when you come back!" But I wasn't willing to let her go so easily. Once back in the UK, I wrote to Ms. E. every week, until finally, early one morning when my mother was getting dressed for work, the phone rang. It was Ms. E., crying and begging me to return. It was great to hear her, but I had to cut the call short, because my mother had to leave for work right away, and the only phone was in my mother's bedroom.

Ms. E. thought I was being abrupt and uncaring to her when I quickly ended the call. When I returned to Miami, I ran into Ms. E. and she said she was in a new relationship.

Despite knowing that my father's health had been declining, it still came as a shock when he passed away later that year. When I was back at the university in

Miami, a police officer pulled me out of class, with an urgent message to call my Uncle Mick in New York. I knew my world was going to fall apart as I raced to a public phone, where my uncle told me what I expected to hear: "I have some bad news, John. Your father passed away yesterday."

Uncle Mick offered to pay my airfare back to the UK if I could make my own way to New York. On the plane to London, I couldn't stop crying, though my uncle remained calm; it was the first time I'd dealt with death and I took it hard. Despite my father's ongoing illnesses, I felt he was taken before his time. My mother was more stoic about it, appearing to take her husband's death in stride, but I knew that she felt the pain as much as I did.

The whole thing made me think about how I had been torn between love and family. It may sound crass, but you only have one father. I think I made the right decision. It's like being on the *Titanic* with only one space left on the lifeboats: do you save your mother or the wife of your young children? Your mother is screaming at you to save your wife, but your heart is telling you to save your mother. Of course, you must save your wife in that situation, and your mother knows and accepts that. Sometimes there aren't any easy choices, and you have to do the best you can.

About halfway through my four-year degree, the university called me in to discuss my degree requirements. They weren't sure what direction I was headed and told me that I could no longer arbitrarily take courses; I would need to declare a major and a plan. I didn't like being told what to do, but if I wanted to stay there, I needed to follow the rules. University is like the Army or any other environment in that regard. You do what you have to in order to get by.

I did eventually graduate with a Bachelor of Arts in Liberal Studies. I figured this would be a key to securing my future and earnings potential, since just about every job required a degree at that point—even jobs like Sanitation and Waste Management Engineer, a.k.a. a janitor. But the degree didn't help me much. I had higher expectations after receiving my diploma.

I later realized that part of the problem was I expected the degree to open doors for me—but it's not a magic piece of paper. It's only worth the work you put into getting it. Liberal Studies was a major for people who had no idea what they wanted to do, and everyone knew it. In short, it wasn't taken seriously by most employers, so it didn't help me much. In addition, by the time I graduated, almost everyone seemed to have a degree, which tended to discount the value of obtaining one.

It helps if you love what you do

I finally found something that interested me. It was for a Comprehensive Employment and Training Act federal government program, which administered funds to local organizations. The recipient of the funding was the Catholic Service Bureau (CSB) in Miami, Florida. One person chosen by CSB would then hire all the 30 people needed to run the operation. I was chosen to be the Assistant Coordinator under an ex-Air Force Colonel. Our mission was to maintain 58 institutions throughout Miami-Dade County.

After the colonel and I had hired all the tradespeople needed, I immediately went to the CSB accounting office and requested that they issue checks for two weeks from their starting date. They protested, saying that the men hadn't done anything yet. I knew that if there was any delay with the first paychecks, I'd be back to square one with no workers again. And I also knew how slow some offices could be. So, I pushed early, and made sure my workers would get their first checks on time, to prevent any unpleasantness.

I set about keeping all these men busy by having them clear a huge piece of mangrove swamp. It was a nearly impossible task without heavy machinery and bulldozers, but I knew that it would keep them busy for at least two weeks. The colonel and I went out there to inspect them and noticed one Cuban man was swinging his machete wildly as if he was trying to kill the bushes. The colonel explained that for every swipe he made, the recently escaped Cuban imagined that he was attacking Fidel Castro. That's motivation for you, I guess—whatever works.

Meanwhile, the colonel and I visited all the 58 institutions to assess their needs. We weren't there to fix everything, but what we could fix, we did. There were not any computers for us to create spreadsheets and schedules, so everything was organized manually. We had a large positioning board on the wall, just like you see in the World War II movies, except we positioned men, not planes or ships. We knew the exact location of every man and what they were doing. An amazingly simple, but effective system. Gradually, CSB came to trust in our capabilities, and the workload increased in magnitude.

The director of CSB was Monsignor Brian Walsh, a tough-talking Irish priest who spoke Spanish. He completely understood the plight of Cubans and their struggle to regain their homeland. He appreciated that we were giving a lot of Cubans a chance to work and improve their lives. The director and I got on well, despite his Irish temper, so well, in fact, that I was even willing to overlook the fact that he was a priest. My early experiences with priests and nuns hadn't been good.

Not everybody appreciated the fact that I got along so well with the boss. When the deputy director, Mr. F.B., found out that I was speaking to the director directly, he told me that all further communication would go through him first.

Well, those were the rules, so I stopped giving Monseigneur Walsh daily updates. But then he started sending me messages, requesting my opinion on this or that. I wrote back, of course. If I was breaking the chain of command, so be it; I enjoyed breaking the rules and getting the job done without adding further layers of bureaucracy.

CSB did a lot for the community in the Miami area, but it had a strange relationship with a local business:

Bacardi, the rum company, which had its headquarters in Miami. There was historically a connection between Bacardi and Cuba. As a result, the rum company maintained close links to CSB and Monsignor Walsh. I'm not sure if this was because Bacardi liked the Catholic Church so much because of what they did for the Cuban cause, or because the priests, nuns and lay workers liked what Bacardi rum could provide for them year-round.

Whatever the reason, Bacardi generously provided drinks for CSB staff, and the rum and wine flowed for all in attendance at frequent CSB social events. I was lucky enough to be invited along with the colonel, to make sure that nothing was wasted. I had no complaints at all—since Vietnam, I'd been drinking a lot more than I used to. Being on friendly terms with a major liquor company may not have been the best thing for me, but what are you going to do? I sure wasn't going to turn down free drinks.

At one of these events I got talking with the Monsignor who, as an Irishman, enjoyed a few sips of the holy water himself. I wanted to tell him a joke since he appeared lubricated enough to hear it, but I wasn't sure if he would get offended. He insisted that he wouldn't. So, I told him the old joke about the priest and the prostitute, which went something like this:

> *"Have you heard about Mary?" said the woman to the priest.*
>
> *"No," said the curious priest.*
>
> *"Well," stammered the woman, "she's a pro…"*

"She's a what?" said the priest.

"She's a pro, pro, prostitute," said the woman.

"Oh, thank goodness for that, I thought you were going to tell me she was a protestant," said the much-relieved priest.

He just looked at me for a moment, and I was sure I had screwed up. Then he let out a bellow of a laugh, even though he'd probably heard the joke countless times before. I caught a glance of the deputy director, and I could tell that he was steaming at the gills, watching me enjoying myself with the director.

It was clear that Monsignor Walsh and I were comfortable with each other, and I was quite sure this gave me the upper hand—there was nothing the deputy director, could do about it. Or so I thought. Actually, I had just dug my own grave without realizing it.

Be careful when you turn your back

I soon found out that a woman directly under my command (Mrs. T.) had been meeting with the deputy director, frequently. I, of course, hardly ever spoke with him, because I was speaking directly with his supervisor and didn't need him. In addition, I didn't want to discuss anything with him because he rarely had anything constructive to say. Why would I need a deputy director, when I can go directly to the director and get a decision straight from the horse's mouth instead of an excuse from the deputy?

The colonel then confided in me that the deputy director was plotting to overthrow me and replace me with this woman. I would then have to follow her directions. Unfortunately, there wasn't a lot I could do to prevent this. I decided to outwit Mrs. T. and the deputy director by finding alternate employment first before they could enjoy my humiliation. I found out later from the colonel that after replacing me, Mrs. T. had to be fired because she just couldn't handle the job. The colonel also left shortly afterwards because he was shouldering all the work that she couldn't do. In short, the deputy director had done nothing but sabotage the entire organization, leaving himself without competent help. Revenge was sweet, although I did miss those frequent Bacardi-sponsored gatherings.

A dream job with less than dream pay

Thanks to my experience at CSB, I was soon able to land a job with a nearby property management company. This company owned a thousand apartments throughout Miami-Dade County. My job was to manage these apartments, with 33 personnel at my disposal; I had completely free rein in how I did it.

Even though I loved the job, it didn't pay as much as I wanted or needed. It wasn't just me—salaries were low at the time overall. Employers could and did run roughshod over employees, because of the huge disparity between the supply and demand of the available workforce.

John P. Culnane, Miami, 1978. Remember chrome bumpers?

My responsibilities included arranging all the large contracts such as painting or roofing. This meant that I got to see all the quotes from different businesses. This put me in a unique position, but also a vulnerable one if I chose to succumb to temptation. Once, one of the roofing contractors invited me to lunch, which should have been a red flag. He asked me how I liked my job there, and would I like to also work for him? I had a gut feeling what was coming next and I was right. He wanted me to tell him the names of the companies bidding, along with their prices; if he won the bidding, I would get a "commission." I told him flat out that I couldn't do that. To me, this was an out-and-out bribe, and I wouldn't do it. I made an extra effort to secure additional quotations for that job. What's more, when it came time to give them all to my boss, I withheld that roofer's bid, so there was no way he could get the job. He even called me to find out the progress, and I told him another roofing contractor, with a better price, had outbid him and got the job. I have my values, and I don't need someone else to change them for me.

I wasn't willing to take payoffs from other companies for handing out contracts. But it occurred to me that serious money was to be made in doing the contract work. I talked to my boss about this and suggested that I myself bid on a large painting contract for 225 apartment units. He initially declined, saying that I already worked for him. But I persisted, and he finally told me that if I got a license and came up with a quote, we could talk about it. So, I continued working for him while I set up an independent painting contractor business on the side. I got a tiny warehouse storage unit with a business address that went with it and had some letterhead printed with my new official legal company name: Southern Painting Contractors. All I had to do now was to give my boss a job quote like everyone else. Of course, I knew what the other contractors were bidding because it was my job to know.

Feeling smug and confident, I gave my boss a quote from my own company that was just under the price of the others. He looked at it and said, "John, I'm not going to pay that much. Look over your figures and bring it back tomorrow." My heart sank, and I thought that I had wasted all that time and effort and money only to have it immediately rejected. But I came back the next day, with revised figures, and he said the words I wanted to hear: "When can you start?"

When you climb a ladder, make sure you trust the person holding it

New painting contractors don't usually start with a 225-unit apartment building. Usually you start small and work your way up. I had some advantages, however, including a smart and crafty boss with an interest in helping me succeed. He conveniently set me up with credit at a local paint manufacturing company. I went back to my old place of work at CSB and cherry-picked the best workers at a fair rate of pay. Now I had financial flexibility and a workforce. I officially left my job as manager and was ready to start as my own boss.

At first, things went great. Two weeks later, I was painting this massive two-story building, and getting my first advance check working for myself. My ex-boss then offered me the opportunity to paint another building, which I gladly did. In all, I eventually painted most of his buildings and was set financially to purchase high-rise swing stages to enable me to paint twenty-story buildings with ease.

But I found that scaling up my company wasn't so simple; as the size of the business increased, so did the problems. For instance, once I was painting the exterior of a 13-story building in Coral Gables when one of the residents contacted me about getting more paint for the work that had been done inside his apartment. This was news to me since I hadn't authorized any work inside his apartment. My workers, in their spare time, had apparently taken an unofficial side job, using supplies from my company without my knowing. They had done a great job of repainting this man's entire apartment—with my specially prepared and expensive exterior paint.

Now, I had a problem. We were in the middle of painting the building. If I fired these guys immediately, the work would come to a standstill. I waited until we had finished painting the building, and then I fired them. I then put a mechanic's lien on the unit painted by the workers, for the same amount that my workers charged the owner, which I believe was around $400. I managed not to lose any money; although the unit owner ended up paying twice, which was not my fault.

Later I told my remaining workers what had happened and warned them that if it happened again, they wouldn't be so lucky because they would be charged with theft. They were as good as gold, and as far as I know, it never happened again.

Things continued to get tougher as the business became larger. I became so busy that I delegated the hiring and firing to a trusted working foreman and paid him accordingly. But eventually I learned that several workers were complaining that in order to get hired, they had to pay him a bonus. No matter how careful I was, it seemed that someone was always trying to out-smart me and game the system.

I tried to remain one step ahead of them. In this case, I followed my usual procedure and got rid of the cheating foreman at the end of the job by telling him I was overstaffed. He continued to call me for work, but none was available when his name came up. He never knew what I knew, but I knew what I knew, and what I knew was that he would never work for me again.

And then there was the painter who was "constantly hungry." I was told he repeatedly took his lunch box outside to his car and came back to the worksite. The work I was doing happened to be for a friend of mine who was a general contractor. This friend called me and told me that about $500 in locks had gone missing and that my painter had been seen near the locks when they went missing. I now had a fairly good idea what was in his lunch box during all these trips outside.

No one could prove that my man had stolen them, but I'd had enough. I pulled him off the job and gave him his final paycheck on the spot. He must not have figured out that I was onto him, because later he even had the nerve to call me back and ask if I had any work. Not only that, but he used me as a reference when applying for a different job. When these people called me for the reference, I changed my voice to sound like a robot and gave him a glowing recommendation. I'm sure they got the message because he didn't get the job.

I bought new replacement locks from a wholesale lock-smith, and just wrote it off.

Work conditions were hard as well. On yet another high-rise building, my crew were dragging their heels, or so I thought. "Why don't you show us how it's done, John," they said. I figured, sure, it would be easy. I put on some old clothes and inched my way up on the electric scaffold high off the ground. With a roller in hand and some extremely pungent primer, I coated the walls for several hours, feeling lightheaded from breathing in all those chemicals. Coming down, I said, "You see, that's how it's done." Their response was, "John, try doing that every day for eight hours." I admitted that I didn't feel great and had nothing else to say. Instead I went home to recover from inhaling the primer fumes; it took me a week to recuperate from massive headaches, a sore throat, and backache.

Eventually, it all got to be too much to handle. Most businesses have peaks and troughs. Painting was no different. I ended up with huge debts on paint supplies and not enough work. I thought I was handling things okay, but obviously I wasn't, because I ended up losing my business, my warehouse, my apartment—even my phone lines were all cut. My car was nearly repossessed—I only kept it because I hid it around the corner when the repo men came.

It was a lady friend who helped me get on my feet again: my savior Barbara and her family took me under their wing for several months. Despite the business problems, I still made sure I had time for the ladies, and

Barbara and I were more than friendly. When I lost everything, she took me to her parents' house in Miami, fed me—even gave me pocket money. When I asked her where the cash came from, as she didn't work, she said every week her father came from the bank with a stash of $20 notes and stuck them in a drawer. She told me her father never counted the money, he just replenished it. I told her that I couldn't accept that, and she assured me that in the future she would withdraw money from her own account instead. I didn't believe her, but I didn't have a lot of choices. I kept my mouth shut, enjoyed my time with Barbara, and took the money.

Each weekday around noon, Barbara excused herself for about an hour and reappeared with $5 in her hand that she handed to me. One day, she invited me to go with her to the bank. We were sitting around for nearly thirty minutes and I asked her why she hadn't even been to the counter. "Just watch," she said. Suddenly, she jumped into the long line and came back with $5.

"The bank gave me $5!" she exclaimed. "Of course, they did, it's your money," I said. "No, John, that's where you're wrong. It's their money, not mine." I must have had a look of puzzlement on my face. "Let me explain," she volunteered. "The banks are now paying about 6% interest on savings and competition for new customers is fierce." Barbara showed me a small sign in the bank that stated if account holders must wait for more than five minutes, the bank will either deposit $5 into their account or give them $5 cash. Barbara chose cash every day of the working week. I was really impressed. "Wait till we go to the supermarket," she said excitedly. "They give me a half a gallon of ice cream for waiting over five minutes in line." I needed a business partner like her.

What you write could last forever, so choose your words wisely

Barbara was a lifesaver, but I couldn't stay at her place forever, living off cash that her father mysteriously dropped off from time to time. I needed another job, and preferably one that wouldn't force me to deal with untrustworthy employees and piles of debt. I wanted something different, something I could do locally.

When I left Barbara's house, I moved into a cockroach-infested trailer that was rented by Arno, a Brazilian, whom I knew from my previous days as a painting contractor. Arno was noticeably quiet, but this was probably since he drank beer from the time he woke up until the time he crashed into his bed late at night.

I couldn't leave any beers in the fridge because Arno and his friends would just consume them, regardless of what I said. I stored them in my cockroach-infested room and drank them warm when I wanted to.

The rent was cheap and there was no deposit, utilities, or expenses to be paid other than my food and gas.

It was right next to a federal prison in Miami, so close that we could hear the loudspeakers addressing the inmates. Sometimes, the television would pick up radio chatter from the guards and we even knew when they would be eating and when lights out was. No need for an alarm clock; the federal prison had everything worked out for you.

But all was not hunky-dory in paradise. Arno had a mean streak lurking beneath his pockmarked skin. Arno had not been paying the rent to the owner, even though he'd been collecting rent from me. One day I noticed a rent possession notice stuck on the front door. I brought this to his attention, and he insisted that I pay him the next month's rent, which was due immediately. I refused to pay him what I knew would only end up in his pocket. He started throwing things around, so I just packed up and left.

Because I didn't pay him what didn't belong to him, I was able to find another place right away. Even though I was broke and destitute, I never gave up hope or allowed myself to fall into depression. When I wasn't sending out resumes or going on job interviews, I watched every soap opera that television had to offer, even when I hated them. Nothing was going to distract me from my focus on gaining employment.

Although my resumes were directed at professional well-paid positions, I was willing to take any job to pay the bills. The problem was few employers wanted an overqualified person for a job they felt I wouldn't be satisfied with. It always ended with, "we'll let you know." Why don't they just tell you "No" there and then? Instead they force you to waste your time by the phone that never rings—or when it does ring, it's a debt collector trying to squeeze blood out of a stone.

I spent some time as a chauffeur, which didn't pay well, but at least had the benefit of some entertaining passengers now and then. Once, when I was driving a sleek Lincoln Continental town car with dark-tinted windows, I was about twenty minutes late picking up a customer. When I arrived at his large house, he barked, "You're late." From previous trips on my own, I knew that this car could get up to 108 mph. When we got on the turnpike, I decided to let it rip. The speedometer hit 90 and then 100. I looked in the rearview mirror and my passengers were glued to their seats as if they were blasting off from a space shuttle. I could see their white-knuckled hands clenched firmly as if prepared for death by lethal injection. They said nothing. What could they say—"Slow down, we want to be late"?

Halfway to the airport, I saw a Florida Highway Patrol car pass me on the other side of the divided highway. He obviously knew that I was flying, but there was nothing he could do. He couldn't record my speed because of the concrete barrier, and he couldn't turn around for about ten miles. Without much time to spare, we arrived at Fort Lauderdale airport. When my passengers left, they didn't say anything, but the expressions on their faces told me that they were either glad to arrive alive or glad to arrive on time—probably both. With a straight face, I just said, "Have a nice day."

On another occasion, I was taking a passenger to Miami Airport. He only had one bag on a large cart at the hotel, which I thought strange. Why didn't he just carry the bag himself? He didn't look like an airline pilot, but the bag resembled the kind of bag airline pilots carry, except much taller. Since I had nothing better to do, I would often speculate on what kind of person my passenger was. I was wondering this when I attempted to pick up the bag.

First, I tried with one hand, then with two hands, but the bag remained firmly on the cart. Finally, I was able to get the bag on my knee and then into the trunk. When I arrived at the airport, I stood at the curb with my hands folded and let the skycap remove the bag. I almost had to hide my face because I was ready to laugh. I had a strong suspicion that the specially designed case was filled with gold; how else could it be so heavy? It must have weighed at least a hundred kilos. The passenger just smiled, knowingly, and placed a C-note in my hands. It was almost worth getting a hernia.

But whereas being a driver had its interesting moments, it had a lot more uninteresting ones, along with long hours and low pay. I turned to journalism. Reading and writing had been my constant companions since an early age. It seemed like a good fit and was the sort of job that someone with a range of office experience and a Liberal Studies degree could get.

I managed to find work as an independent staff writer on an international journal in Miami. The position suited me fine, because the schedule was flexible, there were no backstabbing co-workers, and the pay was certainly better than nothing. I handled regular assignments in business, economy, arts, and politics;

I also got to write editorial pieces, where I was given absolute discretion.

But even though the job was great, it had similar paybacks to my other jobs—low pay and long hours. Gone are the days when employees worked for a large corporation for life, received a gold watch upon retirement, and a pension you could live on. Now employers work you to death for several years while giving you a fancy title with promises of senior management, and then when they have burned you out, they say, "Sorry, John, it didn't work out—good luck with your job search!"

I hardly ever went into the office because most pieces for publication were transmitted by floppy disc or microcassette for transcription the next day. There was no time to waste and certainly no opportunity to change the piece once it had been sent, unlike today when pieces can be constructed on the fly by electronic means. If you needed extra time, you were told, "Perhaps you should work for *Encyclopedia Britannica*, where writers would have a complete year to finish their work! Needless to say, no one complained. If you didn't like it, you knew where the door was.

When I started as a journalist and photographer, there was no internet, no cell phones, and no digital cameras to make your job easier. For the photoshoots, we would take a roll of expensive 1000 ASA fast film, shoot a few frames, get them processed and reuse the remaining unprocessed frames. This way we didn't have to waste a whole roll of 35 frames on one shoot. And if you were unlucky enough to get a bad shot, the piece might not get a photo displayed, which didn't go down well. Sometimes while shooting the photos, people would ask me to be their wedding photographer, but that was a different kind of photography that required a separate set of skills and equipment that I was not ready for.

I once wrote a piece about a flourishing business run by a 49-year-old woman. Naively, I agreed to let her see the piece before publication. In a subsequent phone call, she said she liked it—but when the piece was published, I saw there was a change: the article now left out her age. I called the publisher, who said the woman had called and requested that her age be omitted. After that experience, I never allowed anyone to preview anything. Once you disclose something to me, I don't like being censored.

By coincidence, the office was holding a party the evening before I was due to fly out to London on vacation. Since I seldom went into the office to interact with my colleagues, this was a good opportunity to bond and become more familiar with them. Of course, when my glass was empty of rum, I readily agreed to refill after refill. What I didn't realize was that this wasn't 40 proof Bacardi that I was used to, this was 160 proof heavy-bodied Jamaican rum, and I was knocking it back, straight, like 7 Up.

About 11 p.m., I staggered to my car and started driving. Very quickly I realized that I was completely drunk and could hardly see the road. I pulled over close by, walked back to the office and asked them to call me a taxi, much to their amusement. I was lucky I didn't get into an accident or pulled over for drunk driving. The next day I got on the plane to London and put all of that behind me, despite the headache.

The US Veterans Hospital saved my life

Things really changed when I got a diagnosis that turned my life upside down.

Since I was a US Army Veteran, I was entitled to lifelong medical care and all the benefits under the "GI Bill," of which I readily availed myself. Every year, I had all the usual medical checks done, but this time something was different. Sometime after my annual checkup, I received a registered letter from Veterans Affairs, the office that handled medical testing and procedures, scheduling me for an urgent appointment.

I sensed something wasn't right because they had never done this before. Gritting my teeth, I entered the office and inside were two white-coated doctors and a nurse. They said, "We've run a prostate-specific antigen test on you, Mr. Culnane, and it's come up on the high end of positive. We want to do a biopsy on you." The silence in that room was deafening. I could hardly speak. The doctors said that it was too early to come up with a definitive conclusion of cancer, but after the biopsy, they should be able to tell me more.

I had to sweat it out for a whole week waiting for the biopsy to be done. I was drinking heavily and couldn't sleep. After the results of the biopsy were available, I was again summoned to the doctor's office.

This time they had somber looks on their faces, and one of the doctors put his hand on my shoulder. I knew at that point that my life was going to change, and not for the better. "Mr. Culnane," the senior doctor said, "we have found cancerous tissues in your prostate, and we highly recommend that you take action on this."

My head was spinning so fast that I could hardly take in the magnitude of what they were saying. They brought me a glass of water and explained all of the options available to me. I could ignore it, and it might go away, or at least not get bigger. The second option was to remove the cancer completely with a radical prostatectomy, which essentially means removing the whole walnut-like organ.

This wasn't going well, or anything like I expected.

"So, you're going to castrate me, and leave me with a willy that doesn't work," I exclaimed loudly.

"No, it's not like that," the doctor tried to explain.

"Then how the hell is it?" I said, raising my voice.

He saw that I was upset and offered me a sedative to calm me down. But this decision was too important to make under the influence of drugs: I wanted a clear head.

"Take your time and think it through," the doctor said. "But you do realize that if you just let it go, it might be fatal."

That stopped me. I didn't want the operation, but I wanted to live. And above all, I was a survivor.

"I don't want to die," I said finally.

"In that case, you need to choose surgery right away," said the doctor.

"Let's do it," I said.

Surgery is never as simple as doctors make out. It's like buying a car: there are tons of options to choose from. Make the wrong choice, and you could end up with a pink convertible. In surgery, you stand to lose more than your prostate if they get it wrong.

You might be wondering, how can they get it so wrong? The operating surgeon told me that he would remove both bundles of nerves to prevent the cancer from spreading. When I asked him why he would do that, he simply said, "Why wouldn't you remove both bundles?" But I didn't know what that meant.

I found a book on prostate cancer written by a well-respected medical doctor. It explained that the nerve bundles help a man function sexually. It stated that one bundle can be removed, and the patient can still possibly function sexually. If, however, both bundles are removed, the likelihood of having an erection was close to zero. Or, in other words, you're a dead duck. I didn't like the word "possibly," but given those choices, I'd take "possibly" over "dead duck" any day.

I called the operating surgeon after I had read the book to schedule the operation. But when it came time for the surgery, he had been replaced by the chief of surgery. I spoke with the replacement chief surgeon, and he reassured me that it was unnecessary to remove both bundles in my case.

And on the day of the surgery, he was true to his word. Unfortunately, I never regained my ability to have an erection, despite their valiant efforts to restore my function. Of course, sex is not what life is all about, but it's like eating cake—it's nice to have some icing on the top. I had to relearn how to eat cake without the icing. Now, whenever I eat cake, it's always without the icing.

The final chapter of my American story

While I was fighting my health battles in Florida, my mother was fighting her own battles back in the UK. She had several minor heart attacks and developed symptoms of Parkinson's disease. I was constantly getting emails and calls from friends, relatives and social workers telling me that my mother needed me with her. But I couldn't just up and leave everything in America.

Then one day my mother called me and told me that her carer warned her that the local council might take her house away from her and put her in a care home. This got my attention. I called the council government office anonymously to check the story, and they basically told me the same thing.

Armed with this knowledge, I decided it was time to retire from my life in Florida and return to London; I did not want my mother placed in a care home. She told me, "I don't want to go into one of those places, it's full of old people with grey hair!"

It was strange to return to the UK, but I was happy to be with my mother. We enjoyed many weeks together, with me helping care for her, allowing her to remain in her own home. It was an all-too-brief span of weeks, but a good one.

Several months later, my mother and I went to dinner at a neighbor's. It was a nice evening, capped off with one of my mother's many stories. When it was time to leave, the railings on the steps to our house were wet from a light rain.

My mother asked me to wipe down the railings, so I went back into the house to get some towels. When I came out, my mother had collapsed against the front door, to all appearances peacefully sleeping. But she was not sleeping. In a matter of seconds, my mother had gone from laughing and joking to passing away.

On reflection, I remember when my father had passed away in another house, years before; he had been trying to open the door and leave the house. Perhaps my parents were trying to meet each other in another life. One thing I'm absolutely sure of is that I did the right thing coming back to London, since I got to spend three more months with my mother.

PART 5

The World Is My Oyster

This began a new and exciting chapter in my life. After my retirement, for many years, I bought and sold a few houses and rented them out in various parts of Great Britain. I also traded stocks and options with reasonable success. (But now, because of the world economic turmoil, I no longer do that.) My new career enabled me to travel freely whenever I chose and enjoy the lifestyle I wanted. If I wanted to spend a year in Vietnam, I just did it. Friends would ask, "How can you do that?" I told them, "It's easy: you just buy a ticket, get a visa and go." For reasons best known to them, they didn't, couldn't or wouldn't take that step. What's more, I didn't travel alone. I met a lady named Rachel who lived in Beckton, East London, and we became friendly. Then I invited her on a trip to Cyprus. It was the first of many trips we would take together: for the next seventeen years, we traveled the world, visiting Europe, Asia, Africa, North America, Central America, the Caribbean, and South America.

Of course, it wasn't always like that for me. When you have the time, you don't always have the money. Likewise, when you have the money, you don't always have the time. When you are young, money is usually more important than time. When you are older, you know that time is the most important thing you can possess.

Just buy a ticket and go

Traveling with Rachel was always interesting, and frequently took an unexpected turn. Once, when we were visiting Miami, I casually mentioned to Rachel that I'd never been to South America and she quickly responded that she hadn't either. Two weeks later, we boarded a cheap flight to Bogota, Colombia. Like I said: just buy a ticket, get a visa, and go.

South America was an adventure from beginning to end. Flying down to Bogota, I was certain that the airline pilot was going to crash on the slopes of the steep mountain ranges that surround the Colombian capital. At the last moment, the pilot turned the plane to land safely at Bogota, much to our relief, and he got a round of applause from the passengers.

Bogota, like most South American cities, is a city polarized between the rich and poor. The haves and have nots live very separate lives in separate communities. We had booked our hotel online. And like most hotels in the area, the star rating is usually one less than claimed. Nevertheless, it was clean. It did seem, however, that one person checked you in, the same person cooked breakfast

Rachel and John, breakfast in Mendoza, Argentina, 2018.

Rachel, Tangier, Morocco, 2019.

and the same person was there late in the afternoon cleaning rooms. If you took your key with you when you left the hotel, your room wouldn't get cleaned no matter how many times you asked. Everybody works ridiculously hard and long hours just to survive.

When you walk around at an altitude of 8,640 feet, many people become dizzy and disorientated. I found myself out of breath after walking only a few steps. Rachel, fortunately, was less affected.

"Wrong John"

I think the altitude must have gotten to me because once, when I had some laundry done, I left my passport in the back pocket of my shorts. Rachel said, "You are the most stupid man I have ever met." I spent the next three days drying out the passport and listening to Rachel telling me how stupid I was. She was mad at me because if my passport had been ruined, the whole trip and schedule would have been set back, not to mention the additional expense of staying in Bogota and the cost of a new passport. "Was I right?" she demanded. "Yes, Rachel." "I'm always right," she responded.

We decided to continue to Cartagena on the coast of Colombia. I was determined to visit the beautiful location shown in the movie *Romancing the Stone*. I didn't find it, though, because it was filmed in Mexico, not Colombia. After behaving like tourists for a week, Rachel suddenly jumped up and said, "Look, John, you can go to Medellin, Colombia for $50." I told her that Medellin was considered one of the most dangerous cities in Colombia. But she wanted to go, so I told myself that there might be some safe areas there. I didn't believe it, though.

I found out that I was completely wrong about Medellin, and everything I thought about the city was outdated; it was safe for tourists in most areas except the favelas, the slums. "You were wrong, John. I'm gonna call you wrong John," said Rachel.

During our time in Colombia, we noticed that everywhere we went, police and military manned all the major street intersections. They didn't cruise around in pairs, while the rest stayed at the headquarters, as in most Western countries. Instead, they maintained a pervasive presence in strength and got to know the locals. There was no such thing as a bank being robbed, because, by the time the robbers got to the next block, they would be shot dead: shoot first and ask questions later! Complete control, but after a while it seemed normal to us.

Colombians love to socialize and that means all of Colombia, after work, goes onto the street. That means lots of music, eating, drinking and getting together in coffee bars. This goes on until the early hours of the morning when things close; after that, you don't want to be walking alone on an empty street. The shutters come down, and the rats come out of their rat holes scavenging for food from the mountains of plastic bags put out by restaurants; only the rich can afford bins. Although everyone is supposed to get a bin, you don't get one unless you pay.

Rachel, Phnom Penh, Cambodia, 2015.

Much as Rachel and I liked Colombia, it was time to continue our South American tour and move on to Lima, Peru. I suggested that we go to Machu Picchu, but Rachel said, "I don't want to walk about a bunch of

Rachel, Faro, Portugal, 2018.

old ruins, I want to meet the people." You guessed it; Rachel got her way.

When you visit a continent as large as South America, it's impossible to see everything. Lima is a very sophisticated city, its residents congregating in its ubiquitous coffee bars, many of them speaking English. Rachel always laughs when I speak Spanish, but it works for me just fine, muchas gracias.

We ate very well in Peru. At the seafront, we tried out a few restaurants and the quality was excellent, but the portions were gigantic. So, we shared the huge portions and still ate more than enough. That, coupled with the obligatory bottle of local red wine, meant we were well stuffed. One night it would be grilled chicken, another night freshly caught fish, none of that frozen fish masquerading as fresh. Rachel knows her fish; she told me that fresh fish have clear eyes, whereas fish that are stale don't. I just eat the fish and don't argue with her.

After a week of gorging ourselves on food and wine in Peru, we were ready to do the same thing in Chile. But before we could do that, we had to pass through Chile Immigration. I was using my British passport since most South American countries did not require an entry visa for Europeans. Americans were less fortunate: they had to pay close to $500 for the countries I visited. It's not technically a visa; they call it a Reciprocity Fee. I don't care what they call it; to me it's still a visa with a fee.

The immigration officer looked at my moldy, water-damaged passport, shook his head and called over a colleague. Rachel gave me a look that indicated I was even more stupid than the most stupid man she had ever met, if that was even possible. The officers mumbled something I didn't hear properly or understand, smiled, and handed me back a stamped passport. I left quickly before they could change their mind.

Welcome to Chile. Santiago is a very modern city laid out on a grid system much like American cities. Chileans are fashion conscious and hugely entrepreneurial. But, like a lot of other South American people, they are ready to boil over with social and economic unrest; the police and military are there to maintain order. Periodically, there are violent protests that end

Rachel, Bodegas Lopez Winery, Chile, 2018.

with casualties and, predictably, the government gains the upper hand, until the next uprising.

Rachel and I went to the main square in Santiago where you can see the magnificent cathedral and museum. We noticed a group of police outfitted with riot gear and clear plastic shields. Of course, we had to take some photos, which they didn't seem to mind. The officers were standing close to each other in a riot stance when one of them opened his shield and invited Rachel to stand next to them.

I quickly got that shot that shows Rachel, all five foot four inches of her, her head slightly above and behind the shield. I wanted to show the other passengers on our tour bus the photo, but Rachel objected, saying that it might encourage others to go back, which might get the officers in trouble. I just kept my mouth shut. Rachel often likes to tell me, "John, you're very good at talking, but sometimes you just don't know when to keep your mouth shut."

Chile is not only about old buildings, statues, or museums. It's about wine too. We found a taxi driver willing to take us to a winery about 47 miles from Vina del Mar on the coast. After being educated about wine production, our group, which by now was salivating, was finally escorted to the tasting area.

After a considerable amount of tasting, we were invited by our host to comment. I said, "I wasn't sure that my palate was sufficiently exposed to that particular red." Whereupon, a brand-new bottle was opened just for Rachel and me, instead of the usual small taster. We left satiated and felt that we had certainly consumed more than the price of admission.

We had taken the precaution of having the taxi driver write down the itinerary of the trip and the price to avoid any nasty surprises. He waited for three hours and took us back. By the time we arrived, I had fallen asleep on the back seat ready for the next adventure.

Chile is a huge country, so we chose to stay close to Santiago. I always like to see the coastline of a country, so I was drawn to the small coastal town of Vina del Mar where the fish is so fresh it's kept in large tanks for your next meal.

To me, a good breakfast consists of eggs, bacon, and hash browns, but in Chile and most other South American countries, you get at least ten different kinds of large cakes to choose from. I didn't know that it was someone's birthday! Too much sugar to start my day. But, after some prodding, boiled eggs cooked to perfection were brought to us.

If you've ever been on a ship where you can eat so much that a crane is needed to lift you off the ship when you leave, then you're beginning to understand how much Latinos eat on a daily basis. But we weren't that greedy, at least Rachel wasn't. If it doesn't move, Rachel will eat it, I'm a lot more finicky.

We somehow pried ourselves away from the restaurants of Chile and moved on to Argentina. We decided to cross the Andes mountain range by luxury bus. This consisted of hours navigating treacherous mountain switchback roads and hairpin passes. Several times I had to be nudged in the ribs to stay awake. Rachel said, "We didn't come on this trip by bus for you to fall asleep; we could've just taken a plane." I just nodded and stared out the window at the spectacular scenery until I fell asleep again.

About halfway through our five-hour journey, we reached the peak of the Andes that also formed the border between Chile and Argentina. The view was incredible with snow-capped peaks and the sun blazing down. The altitude affected me, but not as much as it had in Bogota because my body, by then, had acclimatized itself.

Now we were in Mendoza, Argentina. Home of the fabulous Argentinian wines, not to mention the succulent steaks. Of course, we had plenty of steaks that we did not share with each other. After several days of this steak or that steak, I suggested that we might try something else besides steaks. Rachel became quite indignant and said, "Look, John, this is Argentina, and if I want to eat steak every day, that's what I'll do. You got it?" And that's what we did until Rachel became tired of eating only steaks, and then we got back to chicken, black beans and rice. But we never tired of the region's superior wines.

Buenos Aires, by contrast, is truly magnificent. As you walk the wide tree-lined boulevards, your mind conjures up a European capital. Undoubtedly, the original architects were European, many of them from Italy. Argentinians do in fact consider themselves more European than South American; they even speak Spanish with an Italian accent.

If you took away the signs in Spanish, you would be hard-pressed to distinguish Buenos Aires from Paris. We went to the main square on a weekend, where local shopkeepers set up stalls selling jewelry and clothing. Rachel was fascinated by the "fool's gold," otherwise known as pyrite, and had some custom jewelry made by a local vendor for next to nothing.

She always manages to get the best price for everything she buys; I don't know how she does it. To watch her bargain is a masterclass in itself. She once told me, "No matter how much I want something, I won't buy it unless I get the price I want."

But no visit to Argentina would be complete without watching a performance of the Argentine Tango. In the same square, which was surrounded by restaurants, we saw a continuous stream of dancers who were supported by the restaurants and tipped by the onlookers, us. We thought that this display was more natural than the expensive shows around town. All we had to do was sip on a beer and enjoy the whole atmosphere and of course the dancing.

We decided to take a side trip to Mar del Plata on the coast. It's about 260 miles from Buenos Aires, so we took a train from the old grand Constitution Station. This gigantic station is like a cathedral and well worth a visit even if you don't travel by train. I just couldn't understand why no food was served there, except for coffee and small cakes.

Mar del Plata was not the upscale resort I anticipated, but they did have a good selection of pyrite which Rachel made a beeline for. After a few days of heavy rain and walking around with an upside-down umbrella, we returned to what the locals call BA.

Next was Brazil, or as they say, "Brasil." However, you say it, it's a huge country that deserves more time than we spent. We started with Rio de Janeiro or just Rio. We usually booked hotels in the downtown area of the cities we visited. But this was Rio, and no one stays downtown—it's just not safe, especially at night; but we didn't know that. The restaurants and shops closed at 5 p.m. (how unusual is that?), leaving the streets deserted except for the homeless and desperate drug addicts who would be searching for ways to feed their habit. We ended up ordering a pizza delivery through the front desk of the hotel; the doors of the hotel were firmly locked against outsiders. After two days of the downtown Rio experience, we moved to Copacabana Beach, which was open continuously, catered to tourists, and was reasonably safe. Aside from that, we could eat what we wanted when we wanted.

How the other half lives

We had heard a lot about the favelas and were curious as to whether we could visit them. Several travel agents said that tours were no longer conducted because of the danger of gangs shooting at each other. Just by chance, we found one agent who ran small groups through the slums; we signed up immediately.

We both believed that this was the highlight of the Brazil trip. Our tour guide made a phone call to make sure that no gang violence was happening. We started at the top of the favela and slowly walked down through narrow passageways of uneven footpaths.

On every side, we could see poorly built ramshackle houses. These houses had only thin red brick walls with no steel reinforcement rods for stability. It was easy to see how a wall could be pushed over. Leaking plastic utility pipes down the floor areas connected each house with drinkable water. Enterprising local residents filled up buckets of free water, so their water meters maintained a low reading. A spider's web of electric cables supplied those who were able to pay for service. A dangerous array of bypass hooks and wires dangled from the powerlines for those seeking to reduce their power bills. Nobody cared and nobody checked; this was forbidden territory—the favelas.

These houses were built without planning permission and official registration, which meant that they were either occupied by the owner, rented out, or sold for cash. Unofficial deed documents were then passed down in the knowledge that all their time, effort and money could be swept aside if the government chose to demolish their homes. This rarely happened because the government would then have to rehouse those displaced. So, the favelas continue to exist as an affordable way to survive.

These favelas are controlled by powerful drug gangs. Nothing happens without their knowledge or consent. Even the police don't go in there without massive backup, and then they call the gangs in advance to avoid a showdown. Everything is organized to run like a Swiss watch, most of the time.

Violence, when it does occur, is mostly the result of gangs feuding with each other, rather than tourists being robbed. The likelihood of a tourist being robbed on this tour is zero because the gangs know that we are coming. Most likely they are paid a commission from the tour to keep everyone happy. If a tourist were to wander into the favela unescorted, the locals would feel the heat from the gangs if those tourists were harassed.

It's rumored that gangs pay off the local police. Only they know for sure. People who have loose tongues, sometimes lose their tongues. Others who aim to cause harm to the gangs disappear without a trace. There is a law for the gangs and another law for society and the police. Everyone knows their place and it all seems to work smoothly.

This unwritten code is enforced by vigilantes who seem to operate with impunity. Young kids who shoplift and target local stores are mysteriously found dead on the streets of Rio. It happens so often that it barely gets a mention in newspapers. In Rio, most problems that would result in a call to the police in other areas involve a "fixer" instead. You never break the code and go to the police directly if you want to continue living.

After the excitement of Rio, it was time to explore Ouro Preto in Minas Gerais, Brazil. I had known about this place for years because my friend, Elias Martin, was from that town. I had met Elias in Miami where he operated an auto repair shop among other enterprises. He was one of those "Jack of all trades" kinds of people. Elias also ran a semiprecious stone shop in Ouro Preto where he cut rough stones into recognizable gemstones of value.

In Miami, he showed me a photo of his two women stonecutters. Rather than looking at a bunch of tired old men with beards, Elias made sure that all his female workers were "fit." Elias told me that he wanted the best stonecutters who looked good too. I got the impression that his fit female stonecutters received a lot of hands-on personal supervision.

When we arrived at Ouro Preto I asked a considerable number of people if they knew of Elias. But sadly, I found out that he had passed on years earlier.

When I told Rachel that I was interested in semiprecious stones, she dropped everything she was doing and paid immediate attention to everything I said, for once.

We found some local mines and a tour guide, and descended the mine by a rickety old contraption that resembled a mini train but was more like a funicular railway on a steep path. We gripped the side rails, apprehensively, as we slowly entered the cavernous mine. What we saw was a veritable Aladdin's cave of minerals and accumulated dust. We could see, over the years, where miners had hacked away at the surface and extracted semiprecious stones of unknown quantity and quality.

On the quaint old steep, winding cobbled streets of Ouro Preto, not a new building is to be seen. The whole town has been preserved under the UNESCO World Heritage Site criteria. As you walk around, older men dressed in suits and ties approach you and whisper, "Wanna buy some stones." They encourage you to follow them to a nearby store where they can claim a commission for the introduction.

We didn't need that since the shops were all around us and no guide was necessary. While we did look at some stones, or should I say, Rachel looked at some stones, no purchase was made, at least not in Ouro Preto.

Our last trip in Brazil was to Salvador in the northeastern state of Bahia.

We chose Salvador because it was cheaper to return to Lisbon, Portugal, from there than to fly out of Rio. Additionally, we got to visit the place where slaves were originally brought from Africa to work the sugar plantations, as well as the gold and diamond mines.

We stayed in the old town, which reminded us of Portugal. Of course, it would, because the builders of the old towns in Brazil were from Portugal. The hotel very kindly told us to stick to the streets where the tourists were, and to avoid certain areas at night.

We only had a day left in Salvador before our plane left for Portugal when we saw an intriguing shop full of pyrite and other minerals. Rachel could never pass on pyrite, so we went in. But there was more than just pyrite: in the back of the store there was a large workshop where jewelers customized gold and semi-precious stones.

The owner asked us if we would like to be shown the various cuts and qualities of emeralds, to educate us with no obligation. We readily agreed, and the more we saw, the more we (Rachel) liked. I suggested to Rachel that she select the style of a gold ring and match it with an emerald setting. She said, "No, John, I don't want you to spend your money." I took this to be code for yes, I want this ring to be made for me now.

Three hours later, Rachel walked out of the shop having watched the gold ring with an emerald setting being made just for her. As the ring was being made, we took photos of the process; however, for safety reasons she didn't wear it until we returned to Europe. It was a fine memento from an amazing trip—just one of many we ended up taking together.

PART 6

Choices

Rachel and I had many wonderful adventures together for years, always returning to London afterward. However, that was before things changed.

How much did you say you drink?

My health has always been uppermost in my mind, so I decided to have a full health check with a scan. As part of the checkup, the doctor casually asked me how much I drink. Rachel who had come to the appointment with me, said, "John, tell the doctor how much you drink." I told the doctor the truth: I was going through a bottle of port every two days, and port wasn't the only stuff I was drinking. The doctor almost fell out of his chair with astonishment. The port alone worked out to the equivalent of at least five drinks a day, every day; It was far more than doctors recommended as healthy, especially for a cancer survivor my age.

The doctor said that if I wanted to extend my life, I should seriously consider cutting back my drinking, or even stop drinking alcohol altogether. I left that office thinking that was not something I had wanted to hear. But I looked at my recycle bin at the curb and noticed the large quantity of empty liquor, wine, and beer bottles. Inside my house, there were even more empty bottles, so many that they couldn't all fit into the bin; they were piled on the floor nearby.

That was the moment it all clicked. I took a photo of the mess, to remind myself of that moment. And then and there, I decided to stop drinking alcohol. This was a hard change to make—maybe the hardest thing I've ever done. But, after the doctor's earnest recommendation, I wanted to live as long as I could, and I realized just how long I'd spent using alcohol as a crutch. I knew I could do it. And I did.

I began focusing on my health overall—not only did I stop drinking but I also stopped eating sugar, salt, chocolate, and cheese. As a result of these choices, I feel so much better and have more energy than I have had in years. I have lost around 13 pounds as I eat only vegetables three days a week. I also take 100,000 units of Vitamin D3 once a week on my doctor's advice. This alone has boosted my energy levels to where I feel like a 40-year-old again. I am now three score and nineteen!

What makes a survivor?

So here I am, back in the country of my birth. I feel better than I have felt in years. Now, for the first time, I'm looking back, instead of forward. It's given me some new perspective. All things considered, I've been pretty darn lucky.

By this time, since so many women have come and gone in my life, you may ask why I never got married. The answer I gave to many women who asked me that same question was this: "If you promise not to laugh, I will tell you." They duly gave their promises, and I told them, "I could never figure out what to do after foreplay. Is it like five-play?" One woman did ask me about the five-play, but since I was in a relationship at that time, I decided it best to not try and burn a candle at both ends.

Myself, I never ask anyone why they never got married, because the answer is so obvious—they never found anyone who met their requirements. Not getting married is no more a flaw in our character than deciding not to have children. By not doing so, I have saved the planet by making more resources available to those people genuinely in need of sustainability.

Rachel made an excellent point when she said, "John, do you realize that when you are gone, you'll be extinct, because you have no kids." She told me that the same applies to her. It certainly is a sobering thought.

I've had some bad experiences. I haven't let them rule my life, but I can't deny they happened. While many of the physical and sexual abuses, described in this book, occurred a long time ago, I have chosen to forgive, but not forget. Many of the people involved in these abuses are undoubtedly dead now. It is not my intention, after all these years, to rake them over the coals by naming and shaming them. I am neither a policeman nor God.

So, there you have it, the good, the bad and the ugly. If you enjoyed this book and it has encouraged you to examine your own life, and I hope that it has, drop me an email and let me know with your comments. Just remember, it's never too late to make the changes that will improve the quality of your life, no matter what anyone might try to tell you to the contrary.

I especially enjoyed recounting my travels with Rachel. As a result, I'm considering the possibility of writing some more books featuring Rachel and myself on some of these worldwide adventures. If you think I should do this, please contact me, and let me know your thoughts.

To contact the author:
author.johnpculnane@gmail.com
www.johnpculnane.com
https://johnpculnane.blogspot.com

Printed in Great Britain
by Amazon